Accrual Budgeting and Accounting in Government and its Relevance for Developing Member Countries

Sarath Lakshman Athukorala
Financial Management Specialist
Asian Development Bank

Barry Reid
Consultant

Asian Development Bank
Regional and Sustainable Development Department
Governance and Regional Cooperation Division

© Asian Development Bank 2003

All rights reserved. No part of this publication may be reproduced, stored in a retrieval system, or transmitted, in any form or by any means, without the prior permission in writing of the Asian Development Bank (ADB).

This publication was prepared by consultants and staff of ADB. The findings, interpretations, and recommendations are those of the authors and do not necessarily reflect the policies or views of ADB, its Board of Directors, or the governments they represent.

ADB does not guarantee the accuracy of the data included in this publication and accepts no responsibility for any consequences for their use.

ISBN: 971-561-488-4

Published and printed by the Asian Development Bank
P.O. Box 789, 0980 Manila, Philippines

Website: www.adb.org

ABBREVIATIONS

ADB	Asian Development Bank
DMC	developing member country
ESA 95	European System of Accounts 1995
EU	European Union
FMIS	financial management information system
GAAP	generally accepted accounting principles
GASB	Government Accounting Standards Board
GFS	Government Finance Statistics
IAS	International Accounting Standards
IFAC	International Federation of Accountants
IMF	International Monetary Fund
IPSAS	International Public Sector Accounting Standards
MOF	ministry of finance
NAS	national accounting standards
NZ	New Zealand
OECD	Organisation for Economic Co-operation and Development
PRC	People's Republic of China
PSC	Public Sector Committee
RETA	regional technical assistance
SAI	supreme audit institution
SNA	System of National Accounts
TA	technical assistance
UAS	uniform accounting system
UK	United Kingdom
UN	United Nations
US	United States

NOTE

In this report, "$" refers to US dollars.

FOREWORD

The adoption of accrual budgeting and accounting by developing country governments is controversial. Supporters emphasize the benefits and the successful experiences of developed countries. Opponents contend that developing country governments should get the basics right, before attempting to introduce complex accounting practices. In the absence of practical guidelines and reference materials on this issue, the Asian Development Bank (ADB) has generally supported, though not necessarily encouraged, our developing member countries (DMCs) in their efforts.

In doing so, ADB has learned that lessons from developed countries do not always hold true in the DMC environment. In the face of resource constraints, a lack of high-level commitment, complexity and strong opposition from groups with vested interests, ambitious government financial management reform programs often do not fully deliver promised benefits.

This report examines the relevance of accrual budgeting and accounting in government for ADB DMCs and provides relevant background and guidance on this important issue. It presents practical suggestions on how DMCs might improve their government accounting arrangements in a gradual, systematic manner.

This study was completed in early 2003 by Sarath Lakshman Athukorala (Financial Management Specialist, ADB) and Barry Reid (Staff Consultant) based upon their experience in working on related issues in both developing and developed countries in the Asia and Pacific region.

Cedric Saldanha
Senior Director
Regional and Sustainable Development Department
Asian Development Bank

CONTENTS

EXECUTIVE SUMMARY ix
I.   INTRODUCTION 1
II.   GOVERNMENT ACCOUNTING 3
      1. Introduction 3
      2. Differences Between Cash and Accrual Accounting 5
      3. Public Sector Accounting Systems 7
      4. Status of Accrual Accounting and Budgeting in
         OECD Countries 12
III. ARGUMENTS FOR AND AGAINST ACCRUAL ACCOUNTING 15
      1. Introduction 15
      2. Arguments in Favor of Accrual Accounting 15
      3. Opposing Views 23
      4. Conclusion 26
IV.   DMC GOVERNMENT ACCOUNTING 29
      1. Introduction 29
      2. Standards-Based Accounting Countries 30
      3. Soviet Accounting System Countries 33
      4. Conclusion 36
V.   COUNTRY IMPLEMENTATION EXPERIENCES 39
      1. Introduction 39
      2. General Implementation Tasks 39
      3. The New Zealand Experience 40
      4. Implementation Issues and Lessons 47
      5. Conclusion 51
VI.   IMPLICATIONS AND RECOMMENDATIONS FOR DMCS 53
      1. Introduction 53
      2. The DMC Environment is Fundamentally Different 53
      3. Seven Key Recommendations for DMC Governments 56
      4. A Possible Implementation Approach 59
      5. Conclusion 61
REFERENCES 63

Appendixes

Appendix 1.	International Public Sector Accounting Standards	69
Appendix 2.	Government-Specific Accounting Issues	73
	The Reporting Entity and Aggregate Consolidation	73
	Infrastructure Assets	73
	Social Insurance Programs	74
	Valuation Issues	74
	Military Assets	74
	Heritage Assets	74
Appendix 3.	Cost-Benefit Analysis of the New Zealand Adoption of Accrual Accounting	76
Appendix 4.	OECD Implementation Experiences	79
	Canada	79
	Germany	79
	Sweden	80
	United Kingdom	81
Appendix 5.	Useful Internet Sites and Resources	82
	Useful Internet Sites	82
	International Public Sector Material	82
Appendix 6.	Suggested Readings	85

Executive Summary

A general public sector reform trend has seen the governments of most developed countries—including all G7 members—adopt some aspects of accrual accounting as the basis for their budgeting and reporting. There is no evidence that this trend is reversing.

At the same time, the international systems for compiling government finance statistics and national accounts have adopted the accrual basis. Consequently, all major economic statistical systems are now on the accrual basis (for instance, balance of payments).

Moreover, recent studies of developing member countries (DMCs) of the Asian Development Bank reveal that many of their governments are also either moving, or are considering moving, from cash accounting towards accrual accounting.

Supporters of accrual accounting argue that (i) at the aggregate level, accrual-based fiscal indicators provide better information about the sustainability of fiscal policies, provide a stronger basis for government accountability, and provide a better measure of the effects of government policies on aggregate economic demand; and (ii) at the organization level, accrual-based financial statements provide better measures of organizational efficiency and effectiveness, and reduce opportunities for fraud and corruption.

Opponents contend, among other things, that (i) few countries have implemented accrual accounting; (ii) implementation and operation is difficult and expensive; (iii) the emphasis should be on getting the basics right first; and (iv) accrual accounts are more difficult to understand.

Whatever the case, lessons about implementing accrual accounting have been identified from the experiences of developed countries—for instance, the importance of communication, quality assurance, and the use of commercially-available accounting software.

But, DMCs confront obstacles that developed countries do not face: (i) capacity constraints can be overwhelming; (ii) there may be more urgent priorities than improving accounting; (iii) corruption and vested interests can undermine efforts; (iv) donor activities may reduce coherence; (v) reform fatigue may impede efforts; (vi) limited technological infrastructure may reduce options and raise costs; and (vii) supreme audit institutions (SAIs) may have limited capacity. Furthermore, circumstances vary between DMCs, for instance, the Marshall Islands has no professionally-qualified Marshallese accountants in either the public or private sector, whereas the Philippines and Sri Lanka have many private sector accountants.

This study considers these lessons and constraints, and recognizes that for the successful implementation of accrual accounting in a DMC government: (i) implementation strategies and timing should be carefully considered; (ii) political commitment is essential; (iii) intentions and objectives must be clearly communicated; (iv) suitably qualified accounting personnel are necessary; (v) financial management information systems should be appropriate; (vi) SAIs must be suitably staffed and resourced; and (vii) to maximize benefits, the exercise should be part of wider public sector management reforms.

This study concludes that DMCs adopting accrual budgeting and accounting should do so in a realistic and practical manner, as resources and capacity allow. It recommends a gradual step-by-step approach, beginning with implementation of the recently-promulgated cash accounting standard. By doing so, DMC governments will be able to improve their accounting arrangements in a manner consistent with the eventual successful adoption of accrual accounting.

I. Introduction

Many governments have reformed their public sector arrangements in recent years. They want to concentrate on outcomes—such as immunization, literacy and infant mortality rates—rather than the traditional government focus on inputs (e.g., wages, buildings and motor vehicles). At the same time, they are seeking greater efficiency and better fiscal performance.

Accompanying this reform trend is a move for governments to adopt accrual accounting (just like the private sector)—most members of the Organisation for Economic Co-operation and Development (OECD) have adopted accrual accounting to some extent, and more are planning to do so.[1]

In conducting diagnostic studies of developing member country (DMC) accounting and auditing practices,[2] Asian Development Bank (ADB) assesses, among other things, the extent to which DMC governments use cash or accrual accounting. These studies, and discussions with DMC government officials, reveal that many DMC governments are either moving, or are considering moving, from cash accounting towards accrual accounting (see page 29).

At one extreme, supporters of accrual accounting in government argue that "if it's good enough for the private sector, it's good enough for the public sector." At the other extreme, opponents contend that implementation costs outweigh information benefits—particularly for a DMC government.

Implementing accrual accounting can involve significant direct costs in terms of information technology and training, and indirect costs in terms of institutional disruption. Moreover, costs and benefits will vary between DMCs, reflecting their existing capacity, government arrangements and budgeting methods. Nevertheless, in the general

---

[1] OECD. 2000. *Focus*. December (18). p. 1.
[2] RETA 5877: *Strengthening Financial Management and Governance in Selected DMCs* and RETA 5980: *Diagnostic Study on Accounting and Auditing Practices in Selected DMCs*. These regional technical assistance projects (RETA) involved diagnostic studies of DMC accounting and auditing practices.

absence of policies or practical guidance materials,[3] ADB, together with other agencies, has generally supported DMCs in their efforts to improve government accounting.

This study attempts to critically examine the costs, benefits and suitability of accrual budgeting and accounting for ADB DMCs. Its ultimate objective is to provide the basis for a practical and operationally relevant technical advisory note on public sector accounting reform.

This report is intended to support that objective by (i) describing alternative government accounting arrangements and reviewing evidence supporting their efficacy; (ii) examining factors that support, or impede, accounting reforms; (iii) examining and comparing countries that have successfully implemented accounting reforms with those that have not, and the strategies that enabled impediments to be overcome; and (iv) suggesting criteria for evaluating proposed accounting reforms. This report is strictly advisory. It does not represent guidelines or requirements that must be followed in programs, projects or technical assistances.

---

[3] In late January 2003, the following paper was released: Diamond, Jack. 2002. *Performance Budgeting: Is Accrual Accounting Required?* Working Paper WP/02/240. Washington, DC: IMF. The guidance provided by the International Federation of Accountants (IFAC)—IFAC. 2002. *Transition to the Accrual Basis of Accounting: Guidance for Governments and Government Entities.* Public Sector Study 14. New York—concentrates on conceptual issues, such as accounting policy selection and asset valuation approaches. It also includes six paragraphs on transitional and developing countries and three paragraphs on information systems.

II. Government Accounting

1. Introduction

The public and private sectors both used cash accounting until the 16th century. While government accounting remained on a cash basis, the private sector developed generally accepted accounting principles (GAAP)—including accrual accounting—in response to economic pressures:[4]

- the distancing of owners and lenders from managers—driven by the development of financial markets—created a need for better and more transparent information on how well companies were managed; and

- growing competition drove a requirement for better management information on which to base decisions such as price setting.

However, the public sector environment differs from the private sector environment. Among other things: (i) government fiscal activities intentionally impact the economy, for instance, recent US tax cuts are intended to stimulate demand; (ii) government (generally) has power to create money and to coercively impose levies and taxes; (iii) government objectives are broader than those of private sector organizations and include equity, justice and poverty reduction; (iv) in many cases government not only owns an organization, but also is the major purchaser of its goods and services; and (v) governments are accountable to a wider group of stakeholders.

Furthermore, public sector activities are closely scrutinized through the following mechanisms:

- *Budgets and Forecasts.* The executive branch generally prepares annual budgets and multi-year forecasts for scrutiny and consideration by the legislative branch.

- *Appropriations.* The legislative branch (e.g., parliament) generally authorizes the executive branch (e.g., the government) to incur expenditures.

---

[4] For the purposes of this report, the term "accrual accounting" means accrual accounting within the constraints of GAAP.

- *Reports (or outturns).* At year-end, and sometimes during the year, the executive branch generally prepares financial statements for scrutiny and consideration by the legislative branch.

Many governments that have implemented accrual accounting have not uniformly applied the accrual basis to these mechanisms. For instance, budgets may be prepared on a modified accrual accounting basis, appropriations may be made on the cash basis, and reports may be presented on the accrual basis.

This part describes accounting in the context of government structures, which are generally more complex than private sector structures. Figure 1 illustrates common government levels and sectors. Historically, budgeting and accounting methods have generally differed between levels and sectors—for instance, central government agencies might use cash accounting while provincial and local governments, state enterprises, and statutory bodies prepare accrual-based reports.

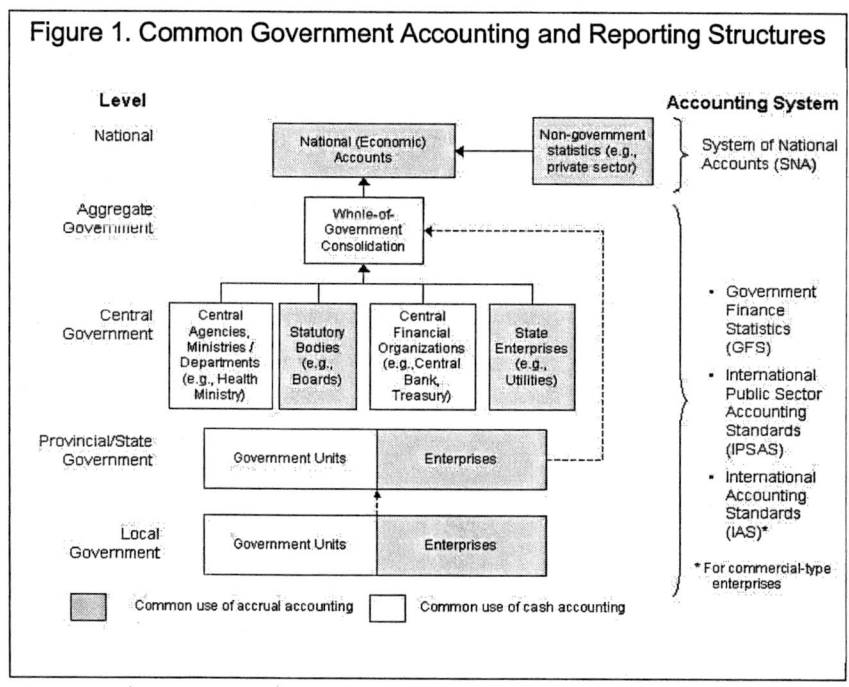

This part provides background information on government accounting. In addition to this introduction, it has the following sections. Section 2 describes cash and accrual accounting. Section 3 discusses the main international government accounting and statistical systems. The status of accrual budgeting and accounting in developed countries is described in Section 4.

2. Differences Between Cash and Accrual Accounting

This section is intended for non-technical readers—it describes cash and accrual accounting, and the differences between the two systems.

- *Cash accounting* records receipts when cash is banked and payments when cash is paid.

- *Accrual accounting* recognizes events and transactions when they occur, regardless of when cash changes hands.

Only a cash flow statement is prepared under cash accounting. Under accrual accounting—in addition to the cash flow statement—two key financial statements are presented:[5]

- *Operating Statement*: Shows the financial results of an organization's activities for a period—that is, were sufficient revenues generated to cover expenses?

- *Balance Sheet*: Shows all financial items the organization owns and owes at a certain point in time, providing insights on the organization's long-term financial sustainability.

Using a simple example, Box 1 illustrates some differences between cash and accrual accounting—the way in which pension obligations are treated is particularly informative.[6] On one hand, cash accounting ignores the $30 million pension obligation (in present value terms) until the pension payments are actually made, usually many years

---

[5] International accounting standards require the preparation of four primary key statements: (i) Statement of Financial Position (balance sheet); (ii) Statement of Financial Performance (operating statement, income statement or profit and loss account); (iii) Statement of Changes in Net Assets/Equity; and (iv) Cash Flow Statement.

[6] In keeping with most government pension scheme arrangements, the example assumes that pension obligations are unfunded.

6   ACCRUAL BUDGETING AND ACCOUNTING IN GOVERNMENT AND ITS RELEVANCE FOR DMCs

later. Conversely, accrual accounting immediately recognizes the obligation as an expense.

Box 1. A Week in the Life of a Small Government

The following example considers a week in the life of a small government. The effects of the following five transactions are shown in the financial statements below:

a. Corporate taxpayers are required to make **tax payments** of $100 million to the government, but only $90 million is received. At the end of the week, $10 million is outstanding.

b. The government **sells fixed assets** for $100 million. The assets had been valued at $100 million.

c. Government **salary payments** are made during the week. In addition to paying employees $60 million, the government is obligated to provide for their pensions when they retire—employees earned $30 million in future pension rights during the period.

d. The government settles a long-running **legal dispute**. It agrees to pay $30 million to the plaintiff in 2 months' time.

e. All the government's borrowings are held in **foreign exchange**. The exchange rate declined by 2% during the week.

Cash accounting would report a $130 million surplus, while the accrual operating statement shows a $30 million deficit. The $160 million difference arises from the fact that cash accounting ignores the pension liability ($30 million), the asset already had a value equal to its sale price ($100 million), the exchange rate change ($10 million), the judgment liability ($30 million), and the taxes to be received ($10 million).

Cash Accounting Information

Cash Flow Statement

Receipts		
Taxation	a	90
Asset sales	b	100
Payments		
Salaries	c	-60
Cash Surplus		**130**
Bank balance		
Opening		50
Closing		180

Accrual Accounting Information

Operating Statement

Revenues		
Taxation	a	100
		100
Expenses		
Personnel costs	c	90
Foreign exchange loss	e	10
Litigation expense	d	30
		130
Accrual Deficit		**-30**

Balance Sheet

	Opening		Changes	Closing
Assets				
Bank	50		130	180
Receivables	20	a	10	30
Fixed assets	700	b	-100	600
	770		40	810
Liabilities				0
Litigation	..	d	30	30
Pension liability	..	c	30	30
Borrowings	500	e	10	510
	500		70	570
Net Assets	270		-30	240
Equity and Reserves	270		-30	240

3. Public Sector Accounting Systems

Background

Government accounting systems determine how financial and statistical information is prepared and presented. The three major international systems have slightly different purposes—Figure 2 illustrates differences in coverage (see also Figure 1 on page 4):

- The European Union (EU), International Monetary Fund (IMF), OECD, United Nations (UN) and World Bank jointly publish the System of National Accounts (SNA). It compiles aggregate financial statistics for an entire economy; government and private sector activities are combined together.

- The IMF Government Finance Statistics (GFS) is a specialized system intended to support public sector analysis. The IMF designed GFS so that government financial information could be compared across economies.

- The International Federation of Accountants (IFAC) began promulgating International Public Sector Accounting Standards (IPSAS) in 2000. They are designed for use in the preparation of general-purpose financial reports by public sector entities (individual government agencies or whole-of-government reports).

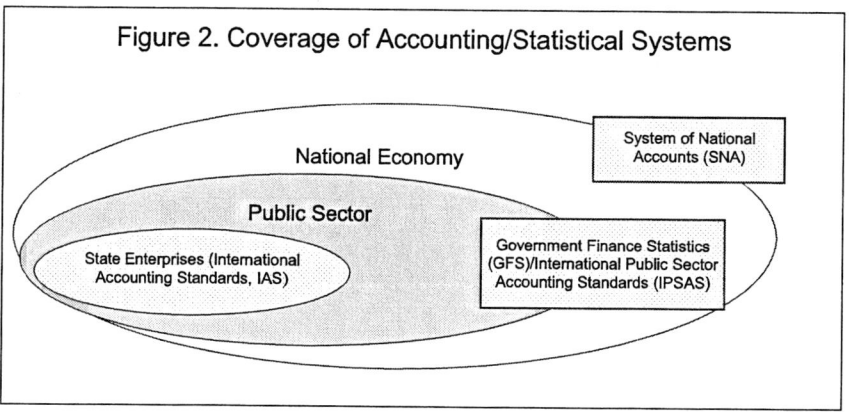

Figure 2. Coverage of Accounting/Statistical Systems

SNA, GFS and IPSAS have been developed, or radically overhauled, in the past decade—all are now accrual based.[7] The European System of Accounts (ESA 95) also mandates accrual-based financial reporting (see page 12). The following subsections describe the three international systems.

System of National Accounts

Most recently revised in 1993, SNA comprises an integrated set of macroeconomic accounts, balance sheets and tables based on a set of internationally-agreed concepts, definitions, classifications and accounting rules. It provides an accounting framework within which economic data can be compiled and presented in a format that supports economic analysis and policy making. SNA is also a reference point for establishing standards for related statistics and harmonizing other statistical systems such as balance of payments, GFS, and money and banking statistics. Furthermore, it allows for the introduction of new accounts such as environmental accounts.

Table 1 presents an example of SNA-based balance sheets. In general, "all the [OECD] government budget and national income account data follows the guidelines of the 1993 SNA."[8]

Developing and transitional economies will require time to introduce the revised accrual system. For example, the Philippines expects to produce SNA-compliant balance sheets in 2003.[9] Sri Lanka expects to do likewise in 2004. The People's Republic of China (PRC) has prepared national balance sheets since 1997, but will not publish these until compilation issues, particularly asset valuations,[10] have been addressed.[11] ADB—together with agencies such as the IMF, UN and

---

[7] In February 2003, IFAC issued a cash-based IPSAS (*Financial Reporting under the Cash Basis of Accounting*). The IPSAS had been approved in November 2002.

[8] Perotti, Roberto. 2002. Estimating the Effects of Fiscal Policy in OECD Countries. Paper presented at the ISOM Conference, Frankfurt. 14-15 June.

[9] Virola, Romulo A. and Estrella V. Domingo. 2001. Changing the Philippine National Accounts Series. Paper presented at the concluding workshop on RETA 5874: Rebasing and Linking of National Accounts Series, held in Bangkok, Thailand, 13-16 February.

[10] Non-financial assets must be recorded at market value, but the PRC values these assets at historic cost.

[11] Lihua, Dong (National Bureau of Statistics). 2001. The Status of Implementation of the 1993 SNA In China. Paper presented at ADB TA No. 5874-REG: Rebasing and Linking of NAS workshop. 13-16 February. p. 3.

World Bank—is supporting DMC efforts to implement the updated SNA.[12]

Table 1. Japan: SNA-Based Balance Sheets: 1996–2000
(Billion Yen)

Item	1996	1997	1998	1999	2000
1. Non-financial assets	3,057,728	3,062,737	2,995,969	2,906,439	2,840,663
(1) Produced assets	1,259,795	1,303,989	1,295,283	1,293,646	1,304,505
a. Inventories	102,703	103,200	98,387	96,788	94,788
b. Tangible fixed assets	1,145,971	1,188,376	1,182,750	1,183,858	1,195,789
c. Intangible fixed assets	11,121	12,413	14,146	13,001	13,928
(2) Tangible non-produced assets	1,797,933	1,758,748	1,700,686	1,612,793	1,536,159
2. Financial assets	5,208,233	5,366,850	5,385,748	5,674,758	5,636,793
Of which shares	425,006	366,721	302,569	502,847	414,493
Closing assets	**8,265,961**	**8,429,587**	**8,381,717**	**8,581,196**	**8,477,456**
3. Liabilities	5,120,883	5,242,263	5,252,475	5,590,023	5,503,746
Of which shares	467,998	402,413	340,436	598,244	482,908
4. Net worth (national wealth)	3,145,078	3,187,324	3,129,242	2,991,174	2,973,710
Closing liabilities plus net worth	**8,265,961**	**8,429,587**	**8,381,717**	**8,581,196**	**8,477,456**
(cf) Historic monuments	245	263	284	303	322
Intangible non-produced assets	116	154	137	194	195

SNA = System of National Accounts.
Source: Economic and Social Research Institute. 2002. *Annual Report on 2002 National Accounts*. Cabinet Office. Government of Japan. 25 June.

Government Finance Statistics

The IMF released a revised GFS Manual in 2001 (see Box 2). In addition to English, the manual will be published in Arabic, Chinese, French, Russian and Spanish. Practical guidance is also being developed.

---

[12] Between 1971 and October 2002, ADB provided $21.81 million to support 60 technical assistance (TA) projects for statistical capacity building (Pant, Bishnu D. 2002. Statistical Capacity Building: An ADB Perspective for a Fresh Approach. Presentation to the ADB / PARIS21 High Level Forum on Statistical Capacity Building for ASEAN Countries. Manila. 7-9 November. p. 16.) See, for instance, ADB TA No. 2875-PHI: *Institutional Strengthening of the System of National Accounts*, for $400,000, approved on 25 September 1997. This TA culminated with a regional workshop in May 2001. Attended by 15 countries from the Asian region, the workshop examined the Philippine experience in implementing and institutionalizing SNA 1993. Individual countries presented papers on topics including preparing consolidated accounts and balance sheets.

The revised manual reflects developments in fiscal analysis. Analysts have traditionally used fiscal statistics to analyze: (i) the size of the public sector; (ii) its contribution to aggregate demand, investment, and saving; (iii) the impact of fiscal policy on the economy, including resource use, monetary conditions, and national indebtedness; (iv) the tax burden; (v) tariff protection; and (vi) the social safety net. However, analysts are increasingly interested in assessing the effectiveness of spending on poverty reduction, the sustainability of fiscal policies, net debt, net wealth, and contingent claims against government, including obligations for social security pensions.

Given these widened objectives for fiscal analysis, the revised GFS Manual has introduced the accrual basis of recording economic events. GFS concepts and principles are now harmonized with those of SNA 1993 so that government finance statistics can be used jointly with other macroeconomic statistics.

Box 2. IMF Releases Accrual-based GFS Manual

"This Manual represents a major step forward in the standards for compilation and presentation of fiscal statistics and thus takes its place as part of the worldwide effort to improve government accounting and transparency in operations. Government finance statistics are a key to fiscal analysis, and they play a vital role both in developing and monitoring sound financial programs and in conducting surveillance of economic policies.

Of particular note is that the Manual introduces accrual accounting, balance sheets and complete coverage of government economic and financial activities. Although only a few countries are currently capable of meeting the standards promulgated in this Manual, the number is increasing steadily and I hope that the trend continues. I commend the Manual to compilers and users as an important instrument in their work and urge member countries to adopt the guidelines of the Manual as the basis for compiling government finance statistics and for reporting this information to the Fund."

Horst Köhler, IMF Managing Director
Foreword to the GFS 2001 Manual

GFS = Government Finance Statistics; IMF = International Monetary Fund

International Public Sector Accounting Standards

IFAC began issuing accrual-based IPSAS in May 2000. They are based on the private sector International Accounting Standards (IAS). Entities applying the accrual-based IPSAS must also prepare cash flow statements in accordance with IPSAS 2 *Cash Flow Statements*. IFAC has issued 20 accrual-based IPSAS (see Appendix 1).

Given their recent and ongoing development, it is not surprising that, as of December 2002, few countries directly referred to IPSAS for their public sector reporting. However, there is a trend for countries to refer to IPSAS when developing government accounting standards. For instance, in designing its government budgetary reforms, the PRC referred to IPSAS.[13] Additionally, the Public Sector Commission of the Spanish Association for Accounting and Business Administration is preparing a conceptual framework for public entities, mostly in line with IPSAS.[14] Furthermore, several international organizations have decided to implement the accrual-based IPSAS (e.g., European Commission, OECD).

Appendix 2 briefly describes selected technical issues associated with the use of accrual accounting in government, including accounting for heritage assets (e.g., monuments), infrastructure assets (e.g., highways), social insurance programs, military assets, and defining the reporting entity.

The Cash IPSAS

In February 2003, IFAC released a cash-based IPSAS (*Financial Reporting under the Cash Basis of Accounting*). It becomes effective for annual financial statements, covering periods beginning on or after 1 January 2004, when a government decides to apply the IPSAS. It has two parts:

- Part 1 specifies mandatory requirements for entities preparing cash-based financial statements, by: (i) defining the cash accounting basis; (ii) defining reporting formats; and (iii) specifying information disclosure requirements. It also addresses several specific reporting issues.

- Part 2 identifies additional accounting policies and disclosures that entities are encouraged to adopt. In particular, it provides guidance on disclosing assets, liabilities and related-party transactions. In doing so, it provides guidance for entities intending to migrate to the accrual accounting basis.

---

[13] Jiwei, Lou (First Vice Minister, Ministry of Finance). 2002. Government Budgeting and Accounting Reform in China. *OECD Journal on Budgeting*. Vol 2(1). December. pp. 51–80.
[14] Montesinos, Vicente. 2002. Government Budgeting and Accounting Reform in Spain. *OECD Journal on Budgeting*. Vol 2(1). December. pp. 333–354.

4. Status of Accrual Accounting and Budgeting in OECD Countries

Table 2 reviews the status of accrual accounting and budgeting in OECD member countries. It reveals that most OECD members have introduced aspects of accrual accounting and more intend to do so in future.

EU member countries are required to prepare government forecasts and financial statements in accordance with the European System of Accounts (ESA 95). ESA 95 uses an accrual-based financial reporting framework to calculate the Maastricht budget balance—the economic and budget criteria set forth in the 1992 Maastricht Treaty. This balance combines all central government departments, social security funds and local government units. However, as the balance does not consider estimated expenditure (i.e., depreciation and provisions), it might best be described as a modified accrual-based measure.[15]

Table 2. OECD Member Countries: Government Accounting

OECD Member	Accrual Accounting for Individual Agencies/ Departments	Consolidated Accrual Reporting	Accrual Budgeting
G7 Economies			
Canada	Since FY 2002	Since FY 2002	Yes
France	Being introduced	Some, full accrual being introduced	ESA 95. Intends to move to modified accrual basis
Germany	Cash statements supplemented with accrual information	No	ESA 95. In preparation
Italy	Yes	Yes	ESA 95. Yes
Japan	Yes	Introducing	No
United Kingdom	Since FY 2000	From FY 2006	ESA 95. Since FY 2002
United States	Since FY 1998	Since FY 1998	Some

---

[15] IFAC. 2003. *The Modernization of Government Accounting in France: The Current Situation, the Issues and the Outlook.* New York. Public Sector Committee. p. 10.

OECD Member	Accrual Accounting for Individual Agencies/ Departments	Consolidated Accrual Reporting	Accrual Budgeting
Other Members			
Australia	Since 1995	Since 1997	Since FY 2000
Austria	No[a]	No	ESA 95. Modified accrual
Belgium	Some	No	ESA 95. Modified accrual
Czech Republic	No[a]	No	No, but will be introducing modified accrual budgeting in accordance with ESA 95
Denmark	Some	Some	ESA 95. Is introducing full accrual budgeting
Finland	Since 1998	Since 1998	ESA 95. Yes
Greece	Some	Yes	ESA 95. Modified accrual
Hungary	Cash statements supplemented with accrual information	No	No, but will be introducing modified accrual budgeting in accordance with ESA 95
Iceland	Since 1992	Since 1992	ESA 95. Since 1998
Ireland	Cash statements supplemented with accrual information	No	ESA 95. Modified accrual
Korea, Republic of	Is introducing full accrual accounting	No	Is introducing full accrual budgeting
Luxembourg	No[a]	No	ESA 95
Mexico	No[a]	No	No
The Netherlands	Since 1994	Introducing	ESA 95. For agencies since 1997. Is introducing full accrual budgeting
New Zealand	Since FY 1992	Since FY 1992	Since FY 1995
Norway	No[a]	No	No

OECD Member	Accrual Accounting for Individual Agencies/ Departments	Consolidated Accrual Reporting	Accrual Budgeting
Poland	Some	Some	No, but will be introducing modified accrual budgeting in accordance with ESA 95
Portugal	Yes	No	ESA 95. Is introducing additional accrual information
Slovak Republic	No[a]	No	No, but will be introducing modified accrual budgeting in accordance with ESA 95
Spain	Modified accrual	Modified accrual	ESA 95. Modified cash
Sweden	Since 1994	Since 1994	ESA 95. Is introducing full accrual budgeting
Switzerland	Yes	No	Is introducing full accrual budgeting
Turkey	No[a]	No	No

ESA 95 = European System of Accounts 1995; FY = Fiscal Year;
OECD = Organisation for Economic Co-operation and Development.

a   Most countries actually use modified cash accounting (for a discussion, see IFAC. 2000. *Government Financial Reporting: Accounting Issues and Practices*. Study No. 11. New York: Public Sector Committee).

Sources: OECD. 2002. PUMA Database Reports. August. Paris; OECD. 2002. *Accrual Accounting and Budgeting: Key Issues and Recent Developments*. PUMA/SBO(2002)10. Paris; Blöndal, Jón R. and Jens Kromann Kristensen. 2002. Budgeting in the Netherlands. *OECD Journal on Budgeting*. Vol 1(3). pp. 43–80; OECD. 1998. *Public Management Developments in Austria: Update 1998*. Paris; OECD. 1999. *Focus*. 12 March; Swedish National Financial Authority (Ekonomistyrningsverket). 2001. *Accrual Accounting in Swedish Central Government*. May. Stockholm. p. 27; Montesinos, Vicente. 2002. Government Budgeting and Accounting Reform in Spain. *OECD Journal on Budgeting*. Vol 2(1). December. pp. 333–354; and Study Group on Explanatory Methods of Fiscal Position. September 2001. *The Japanese Government Balance Sheet* (Preliminary trial). Ministry of Finance. See http://www.mof.go.jp/english/budget/bs/zai003e.pdf [3 January 2003].

III. Arguments For and Against Accrual Accounting

1. Introduction

Part II of this report described the trend—at least among developed countries—towards adoption of accrual budgeting and accounting. This part considers the factors influencing this trend. In addition to this introduction, it comprises the following sections. Section 2 describes the reasons given for government adoption of accrual budgeting and accounting. Section 3 examines arguments against accrual accounting and Section 4 concludes.

2. Arguments in Favor of Accrual Accounting

This section describes the arguments put forward in support of government adoption of accrual accounting. It is based on information from a variety of sources, including ADB, OECD and IMF publications.[16] For reasons already described, governments differ from private sector organizations. In particular, aggregate (whole-of-government) accounting information is used for different purposes from organization-level information (e.g., a government ministry). As such, the first subsection examines accrual accounting at the aggregate level and the second subsection takes the organization-level perspective.

---

[16] Primary sources:
- Diamond, Jack. 2002. *Performance Budgeting: Is Accrual Accounting Required?* Working Paper WP/02/240. Washington, DC: IMF.
- IFAC. 1996. *Perspectives on Accrual Accounting.* Occasional Paper 3. New York: Public Sector Committee.
- IMF. 2002. *Government Finance Statistics 2001 Companion Material.* Washington, DC.
- IMF. 2001. *Manual on Fiscal Transparency.* Washington, DC: Fiscal Affairs Department.
- Mellor, Thuy. 1996. Why Governments Should Produce Balance Sheets. *Australian Journal of Public Administration.* 55(1). March. pp. 78-81.
- OECD. 2002. *Accrual Accounting and Budgeting: Key Issues and Recent Developments.* PUMA/SBO (2002)10. Paris.
- Schiavo-Campo, Salvatore and Daniel Tommasi (eds.). 1999. *Managing Government Expenditure.* Manila: ADB.
- World Bank. 1998. *Public Expenditure Management Handbook.* Washington, DC.

At the Aggregate (whole-of-government) Level

The definition of the aggregate government entity differs between countries and depends on their constitutional and public sector management arrangements. For instance, the United Kingdom (UK) consolidates local government information into their government financial statements, whereas the United States (US) does not. This particular issue (the reporting entity) is described further in Appendix 2.

Among other things, aggregate government financial information should support judgments and decisions on the[17]

- effect of government decisions on *aggregate demand*—for instance, how are changes in the composition of government spending likely to affect overall economic activity, in the short, medium and long run?
- *accountability* of executive government—for instance, to what extent has government delivered on its stated intentions?
- *sustainability* of fiscal policies—for instance, are tax reductions sustainable in the long run (in comparison to changes in net asset / debt levels?

The remainder of this subsection examines the usefulness of accrual-based information against these objectives.

Aggregate demand: measuring the effects of government activities

SNA 1993 provides instructions on preparing macroeconomic statistics, particularly national accounts (see page 8). The publishers of SNA (EU, IMF, OECD, UN and World Bank) contend that SNA favors accrual accounting over cash accounting because (i) the timing of accrual accounting is fully consistent with the way SNA defines economic activities and other flows; and (ii) accrual accounting can be applied to non-monetary flows.[18]

The IMF presents similar arguments in favor of the accrualization of GFS. For example, under cash accounting, the interest paid on a zero-coupon bond would not be recorded until the bond matures, which could be many years after the expense was incurred (see Box 3).[19]

---

[17] Based on papers prepared by the New Zealand Treasury when considering whether government budgets should be accrual-based (New Zealand Treasury. 1993. Reports of the Fiscal Indicators Working Party. Unpublished documents).

[18] UN. 1993. *System of National Accounts (SNA) Manual*. New York. paras. 3.92–3.96.

[19] IMF. 2001. *Government Finance Statistics Manual*. paras 3.47–3.53. Washington, DC.

> **Box 3. Cash and Accrual Treatment of a Zero-Coupon Bond**
>
> Consider a 5-year, $1,000,000, zero-coupon treasury bond that is sold for $700,000. The following example illustrates the differences in treatment between cash accounting and accrual accounting (the interest expense calculation is based on a yield-to-maturity of 7.394%).
>
> | | Year | | | | | | Total |
> |---|---|---|---|---|---|---|---|
> | | 0 | 1 | 2 | 3 | 4 | 5 | |
> | **Cash Basis** | | | | | | | |
> | Cash Flows | 700 | 0 | 0 | 0 | 0 | -1000 | -300 |
> | **Accrual Basis** | | | | | | | |
> | Operating Statement: Interest expense | 0 | 52 | 56 | 60 | 64 | 68 | 300 |
> | Balance Sheet: Outstanding liability | 700 | 752 | 808 | 868 | 932 | 0 * | |
>
> * Obligation is fully paid in year 5, thereby eliminating the outstanding liability.

Furthermore, the IMF contends that separating current and capital transactions is useful for analyzing the economic impacts of fiscal policy. By providing information on depreciation and asset valuation changes, accrual information allows better judgments to be made on the quality of government investments and the sustainability of fiscal policy. It also removes the conflicting treatment of sales of financial equity and physical assets.[20]

Financial information as a basis for government accountability

Government accountability arrangements differ markedly among countries depending, among other things, on electoral arrangements, political institutions and the degree of decentralization. However, these differences are generally not important when considering the appropriateness of fiscal information as a basis for accountability.

More comprehensive. The IMF considers the accrual basis superior "because all resource flows are recorded, including internal transactions, in-kind transactions and other economic flows. This comprehensive recording permits the integration of flows with changes in the balance sheet." In any case, accrual reports also provide a cash flow statement. Conversely, cash-based accounts normally do not differentiate between expenses and acquisitions of nonfinancial assets (such as buildings). Under the accrual basis, acquisitions of nonfinancial assets are recorded separately.[21]

---

[20] IMF. 2001. *Manual on Fiscal Transparency*. Washington, DC: Fiscal Affairs Department.
[21] IMF. 2001. *Government Finance Statistics Manual*. Washington, DC. paras 3.47–3.53.

Simpler and easier to understand. Cash accounts generally comprise a single income and expenditure statement—in contrast to the multiple statements and notes provided by accrual information. In practice, cash-based government financial statements tend to be idiosyncratic and difficult to understand and interpret. Conversely, accrual financial statements are familiar to a wide range of people (e.g., businesspeople, financial journalists and credit rating agencies).[22]

> "...prior to the New Zealand reforms, ... [government] financial statements and budgetary documents ... could not be easily understood even by accountants and financial experts in the private sector ... The [adoption of accrual accounting] changed this dramatically."[23]

Lower borrowing costs. Credit rating agencies are familiar with accrual information through their private sector activities. There is evidence from the US that "states that use accrual information borrow at better terms than those states that use solely cash information."[24]

Harder to manipulate. Both cash and accrual information can be manipulated, but many non-technical people believe cash accounts to be less prone to manipulation than accrual information.

Accrual information can be manipulated by (i) selecting favorable accounting policies; (ii) making favorable assumptions, for instance on discount rates; and (iii) managing accruals. Cash information can also be massaged by: (i) selecting favorable accounting policies; (ii) changing payment and receipt dates: (iii) changing the reporting entity; and (iv) classifying current items as capital items or vice versa (for instance, privatization proceeds might be shown as revenue).[25]

In the absence of independent cash-focused accounting principles, cash information is more easily manipulated than accrual informa-

---

[22] Ball, I., T. Dale, W. D. Eggers and J. Sacco. 1999. *Reforming Financial Management in the Public Sector: Lessons US Officials Can Learn From New Zealand.* Policy Study No. 258. Los Angeles: Reason Public Policy Institute. Reason Foundation.
[23] Campos, J. E. & Pradhan, S. 1997. Evaluating public expenditure management systems: an experimental methodology with an application to the Australia and New Zealand reforms. *Journal of Policy Analysis and Management,* 16(3), 423-445. p. 432
[24] Brumby, Jim in Schiavo-Campo, Salvatore and Daniel Tommasi (eds.). 1999. *Managing Government Expenditure.* Manila: ADB. p. 360.
[25] For further information on creative cash accounting practices, see: Diamond, Jack. 2002. *Performance Budgeting: Is Accrual Accounting Required?* Working Paper WP/02/240. Washington, DC: IMF.

tion.[26] For instance, the 1992 Maastricht Treaty, together with the Stability and Growth Pact, set the basis for the European Economic and Monetary Union (EMU). Several European countries manipulated their cash-based fiscal information in order to achieve the fiscal targets set out in these agreements, To combat these practices, the European System of Accounts (ESA 95) mandated accrual-based accounting standards.[27]

More comparable and consistent. The IMF contends that accrual information improves understanding of the underlying fiscal position by removing year-to-year variability caused by the timing of cash receipts and payments (particularly capital payments).[28]

The revised GFS and the major macroeconomic statistical systems (SNA, balance of payments, and monetary and financial statistics) use the accrual basis.[29] Consequently, preparing government financial statements and forecasts on the accrual basis improves the accuracy of national accounts and economic forecasts (see Box 4).

Box 4. SNA Accounting Basis

"A choice has to be made, recognizing (a) the needs of macroeconomic analysis, (b) microeconomic views, and (c) commonly available sources. Often, in this respect, a distinction is drawn between recording flows on a cash basis, due-for-payment basis and accrual basis. The System recommends recording on an accrual basis throughout."

Para. 3.91. SNA 1993 Manual

SNA = System of National Accounts.

Financial information on the sustainability of fiscal policies

Financial markets and credit rating agencies are particularly interested in the sustainability of financing and expenditure policies. The IMF contends that accrual financial statements provide a richer set of information for analyzing the sustainability of fiscal policy and the quality of fiscal decision-making.[30]

---

[26] Behaviors of the US government in response to Gramm-Rudman-Hollings incentives and those of European governments regarding Maastricht criteria, belie the common belief that cash information is less manipulable than accrual information. For a fuller discussion, see Easterly, W. 1999. *When Is Fiscal Adjustment an Illusion?* Paper 2109, World Bank Country Economics Department. Washington, DC: World Bank.

[27] Buti, Marco and Gabriele Giudice. 2002. *Maastricht's Fiscal Rules at Ten: An Assessment.* European Commission.

[28] IMF. 2001. *Manual on Fiscal Transparency.* Washington, DC: Fiscal Affairs Department.

[29] IMF. 2001. *Government Finance Statistics Manual.* Washington, DC. paras 3.47–3.53.

[30] IMF. 2001. *Manual on Fiscal Transparency.* Washington, DC: Fiscal Affairs Department.

Includes liability disclosures. Governments generally have significant liabilities other than public debt (borrowings). An important example is the future obligation to pay civil service pensions. These obligations are typically underfunded, but—under accrual accounting—the unfunded liability is usually shown on the balance sheet as a liability. Other liabilities include accounts payable, accrued interest and accrued salaries and wages, transfer payments payable, environmental liabilities, and obligations under accident compensation schemes. Under accrual accounting, additional disclosures are made in supplementary notes. These include information on contingent liabilities and on commitments.[31]

Information is provided for considering intergenerational fairness. Intergenerational fairness is important in fiscal policy—it reflects the degree to which the government today is paying the costs of services today, as opposed to shifting costs to other periods. Accrual accounting provides a longer-term perspective for judging policy impacts. For example, without accrual accounting, decisions on pensions that create pension liabilities may not fully consider the impact of the liabilities on future budgets.

Basis for identifying payment arrears. Payment arrears arise when an obligatory payment is not made by its due-for-payment date. All arrears are automatically included in accrual-based statistics. However, additional analysis is required to prepare an analysis of total accounts payable that is in arrears.[32]

Information for managing liquidity. Managing liquidity is crucial to government operations. It is not necessary to use the cash basis to meet this need. Cash flow information is provided by the accrual basis. It may also be difficult to assess solvency and future cash flows with the cash basis because arrears information is missing.[33]

Better information for decision making. Fiscal strategy refers to the direction and objectives of fiscal policy and the management of revenue and expenditure flows, assets and liabilities. Under the cash basis, fiscal strategy focuses on short-term revenues and expenditures (i.e., 1–3 years). Under the accrual basis, assets and liabilities are given the same attention as debt in terms of targets, risk analysis and contribution to economic policy objectives.

---

[31] Ibid.
[32] IMF. 2001. *Government Finance Statistics Manual.* Washington, DC. paras 3.47–3.53.
[33] Ibid.

Box 5 illustrates the difficulty of determining fiscal strategy solely based on cash information. In the Croatian case, relying only on cash information might lead policymakers to tighten fiscal policy through, for instance, reductions in health programs. Contrast this with the US situation. These examples demonstrate that developing countries should be careful in taking decisions based on incomplete information (i.e., on cash information only).

Box 5. Accrual and Cash Information is Complementary

A Comparatively Higher Cash Deficit (Croatia)
"Some of the data published by the MOF may give a false impression of fiscal developments. Since the fiscal accounts continue to be presented on a cash basis, the figures suggest that the deficit rose in 2000 and continued to rise in 2001. But this increase actually reflects the repayment of arrears (i.e., payment of obligations accrued in earlier years). In accrual terms ... the fiscal deficit has in fact been decreasing. In 2002, the cash presentation should not differ substantially from the accrual presentation since the bulk of arrears has been repaid."
— Croatian National Bank (2002)[34]

A Comparatively Higher Accrual Deficit (US)
"Accrual based financial reporting is critical to gaining a comprehensive understanding of the US Government's operations. For fiscal year 2001, our results were an accrual-based deficit of $515 billion in contrast to a $127 billion [cash] surplus reported last fall. The primary difference between the accrual deficit and the [cash] surplus is the recognition of expanded military retiree health benefit costs provided by the National Defense Authorization Act, which was signed into law on October 30, 2000, and other actuarial expenses. In fact, these expenses caused the government's future obligations to its military and civilian retirees to exceed the federal debt held by the public. As with other future obligations of the federal government, only accrual-based financial reporting provides this information in context to the public."
— US Secretary of the Treasury (2002)[35]

MOF = Ministry of Finance.

At the Agency (Organization) Level

This section describes the arguments presented in favor of accrual accounting at the agency level.[36]

---

[34] Kraft, Evan and Tihomir Stucka. 2002. *Fiscal Consolidation, External Competitiveness and Monetary Policy: A Reply to the WIIW*. May. Zagreb: Croatian National Bank. p. 1.
[35] US Government. 2002. *2001 Financial Report of the United States Government*. Washington, DC. p. 1.
[36] Primary source: Ball, I., T. Dale, W. D. Eggers and J. Sacco. 1999. *Reforming Financial Management in the Public Sector: Lessons US Officials Can Learn From New Zealand*. Policy Study No. 258. Los Angeles: Reason Public Policy Institute. Reason Foundation.

Better accountability basis. Accrual accounting is intended to provide information to owners and lenders. The information contained in accrual-based reports is useful both for accountability and decision-making. Financial reports prepared on an accrual basis allow users to assess accountability for all resources the entity controls and how those resources are used.

Provides information for managing resources. Cash accounts exclude most assets and liabilities. Complete records of assets and liabilities are maintained under accrual accounting. This facilitates better asset management, including better maintenance, more appropriate replacement policies, identification and disposal of surplus assets, and better management of risks (such as loss due to theft or damage). Identifying assets and recognizing depreciation helps managers to understand the impact of using fixed assets to deliver services, and encourages them to consider alternative ways of managing costs and delivering services.

Concentrating on cash payments alone may result in an unnoticed deterioration in fixed assets. If major pieces of equipment are becoming obsolete, or long-term liabilities are accumulating, owners and lenders want to know now, not when the equipment is sold or scrapped, or when liabilities come due.

Identifies payment arrears. In contrast to cash information, accrual information provides a basis for identifying payment arrears.

Supports better liquidity management. The richer suite of information provided under the accrual basis, including cash information, represents a sound foundation for managing liquidity.

Provides a basis for pricing products and services. Government is interested in obtaining good quality of goods and services at the best competitive price. Although nonfinancial measures are generally necessary to measure quality, accrual accounting provides information on which to compare price. By contrast, cash accounting is inadequate for pricing because some elements of resource usage (e.g., depreciation) are not fully allocated to costs. Where a government agency is competing to provide goods or services, all costs should be allocated to the goods or services, otherwise prices may be understated and taxpayers will unknowingly subsidize public providers of goods or services. Subsidies or hidden costs make the public provider's price artificially low, which means taxpayers do not get as good a deal as they could with fair competition, and private suppliers may be driven out of the market. Accrual accounting lets virtually all costs be allocated to an output. Cash accounting does not.

A cash-based system does not provide information about total costs of government activities. Only an accrual-based operating statement provides information on the total costs of resources used to deliver government services, which is essential information for government decision makers.[37]

Reduces opportunities for fraud and corruption. The integrated asset management nature of accrual accounting provides greatly enhanced asset stewardship. For instance, it improves control over donor-provided assets. Furthermore, cash-based systems are more easily manipulated than accrual-based systems.

3. Opposing Views

While generally recognizing that the accrual accounting basis is superior to the cash basis, opponents tend to raise concerns about implementation difficulties. But, at the extreme, some commentators appear to oppose private sector use of accrual accounting (see Box 6). This section attempts to present the arguments against the use of accrual accounting in government.

---

[37] Mellor, Thuy. 1996. Why Governments Should Produce Balance Sheets. *Australian Journal of Public Administration.* 55(1). March. pp. 78-81.

> **Box 6. Professor Schick's Views on Enron and Accrual Accounting**
>
> One of the most vociferous opponents of accrual accounting is Allen Schick, a US political scientist. In May 2002, he made the following presentation:
>
> "Shifting the [Government] Budget to the Accrual Basis would not avert an Enron Fiasco[38]
> - Enron reports its finances on the accrual (GAAP) basis.
> - The accrual basis does not remedy the "Off-Balance Sheet" problem.
> - The accrual basis entails numerous, often complex, assumptions about future events.
> - These assumptions are subject to judgment and manipulation.
> - The assumptions often dominate the relationship between firms and outside auditors.
> - It is more difficult for ordinary people (taxpayers, media, etc.) to understand accruals than cash flows.
> - Analysts often rely on cash flows to assess a firm's performance and condition."
>
> However, as a non-accountant, Professor Schick is unaware that (i) Enron took advantage of gaps in country accounting standards to avoid consolidating special purpose entities—this failing was due to accounting standards, not accrual accounting; and (ii) accrual financial statements include cash flow information.

GAAP = generally accepted accounting principles.

Few countries have implemented accrual accounting

To varying extents, most OECD member countries have implemented accrual accounting in the past decade (see Table 2 on page 12). But, only four OECD member countries appropriate resources on the accrual basis (Australia, Finland, Iceland and New Zealand). Others, including Canada and UK, also intend to introduce accrual appropriations. Implementing accrual appropriations generally requires fundamental legal changes. Therefore, widespread adoption is likely to take a longer period (see Box 7).

> **Box 7. Accrual Appropriations**
>
> "Extending accruals to budgeting is controversial. Much of that controversy arises from the government administration itself and Parliaments. Before this change is contemplated, a significant amount of time needs to be invested in educating and consulting with government managers and other interested groups, like parliamentarians. In those countries that have adopted accruals, the change has been linked to other public management reforms. Accrual accounting places a premium on confidence in audits and a willingness to accept fluctuations in valuations. Practice in Australia and New Zealand has shown that the use of accruals in the budget has led to a better realization of future unfunded liabilities, better infrastructure management and a more efficient budget reallocation process."[39]

---

[38] Schick, Allen. 2002. Fiscal Rules and Fiscal Risks. Presentation at the World Bank Training Course. 21 May.
[39] Matheson, Alex. 2002. Better Public Sector Governance: The Rationale for Budgeting and Accounting Reform in Western Nations. *OECD Journal on Budgeting.* Vol 2(1). December. pp. 44–45.

Implementation is difficult and expensive

Some aspects of accrual accounting implementations are more difficult than cash implementations. For example, it is difficult for a government organization to know the full amount of tax revenue that it is likely to receive at a given time.

Moreover, implementing and operating an accrual accounting system can be expensive. However, although millions of organizations use accrual accounting, few use cash accounting. Variations in cash accounting methods between countries further limit the availability of computerized accounting information systems. Indeed, many countries develop their own computer systems to support cash accounting, rather than rely on proven commercial accounting systems (with accrual accounting capability).

In any case, whether a government uses cash or accrual accounting, qualified accounting personnel must manage the system.

Ongoing operation is difficult and expensive

Arguments are made that clerical staff can operate cash-based accounting systems with minimal input from qualified accountants, whereas accrual-based systems require trained accountants, particularly during implementation. However, actual experience does not necessarily support this contention.[40]

Given that the private sector uses accrual accounting, recruitment and training of accounting staff is easier under accrual accounting. Moreover, accrual systems (generally) require fewer personnel to operate them.

The adoption of accrual accounting removes a barrier preventing access of private sector trained financial managers to many public sector financial management jobs. Adoption of accruals means that the public sector can attract properly trained accountants who can put their skills to use. This is important for creating sources of innovation and for removing the monopoly on the knowledge of public agencies' financial conditions from those with limited general financial skills but who have institutional knowledge.[41]

---

[40] *Ibid.*
[41] Brumby, Jim and Marco Cangiano. 2001. Public Expenditure Management Reform and Fiscal Consolidation in OECD Countries. Paper presented at the Fifth International Conference Institutions in Transition organized by the Slovenian Institute of Macroeconomic Analysis and Development in Otočec, Slovenia, 13-14 July.

Emphasis should be on getting the basics right first

There is a view that countries should get the basics right before attempting more advanced reforms, such as accrual accounting. This reflects experience with developing countries whereby extensive, and usually unsuccessful, efforts have been made to strengthen basic record keeping and cash accounting over the past 2 decades.[43]

Accrual accounts are less objective and more difficult to understand

Some argue that accrual accounting is less objective than cash accounting. Under cash accounting, money is either in the bank or it is not. Critics contend that decision makers, policymakers, credit rating agencies, the media and the public struggle to understand the richer suite of information presented in accrual-based financial statements.

Indeed, an accrual accounting environment may support retention of skilled accountants—for instance, the Fiji Islands' public sector accountants supported introducing accrual accounting as a measure to enhance retention of skilled accountants in the public sector.[42]

4. Conclusion

Table 3 attempts to summarize the comparative usefulness of accrual and cash accounting in government.

Table 3. Summary Comparison of Cash and Accrual Accounting

Criteria	Cash Accounting	Accrual Accounting
Ease of understanding	Simpler, but unfamiliar	Greater complexity, but familiar to more people
Ease of manipulation	Relatively easy to manipulate, but the issuance of the Cash Basis IPSAS is a big step forward.	Ease of manipulation depends upon accounting and auditing standards.
Comprehensiveness	Cash information only	Includes cash information together with other information
Usefulness for managing liquidity	Provides only basic information	Provides cash information and commitment information (e.g., payment arrears)

---

[42] Ministry of Finance and National Planning Survey reported in: ADB. 2002. *Diagnostic Study of Accounting and Auditing Practices in the Fiji Islands*. Manila. p. 82.
[43] World Bank. 1998. *Public Expenditure Management Handbook*. Washington, DC. p. 8.

Criteria	Cash Accounting	Accrual Accounting
Non-financial asset management	No information provided	Provides information on asset use
Comparability	Countries use a range of cash accounting bases, policies are generally not explained well Not consistent with GFS and SNA	Countries use different accrual accounting standards Consistent with GFS and SNA
Measuring sustainability of fiscal policy / considering intergenerational equity	Very limited usefulness	Useful, but needs to be supplemented with additional information (e.g., demographic profiles)
Credibility	Limited	Credit rating agencies, lenders and the media are more familiar with accrual financial statements Can lead to lower borrowing costs
Basis for determining fiscal strategy	Limited	Good, in conjunction with cash information
Accountability	Limited	Provides information on accountability for resources (e.g., fixed assets)
Basis for product/ service pricing	Limited	Good
Disincentives for fraud and corruption	Limited	Better than cash, but depends on the internal control environment (among other things)
Implementation	Information system costs can be higher (because of customization and limited availability)	Although information system costs may be lower, additional efforts are required to identify and value assets (among other things)
Ongoing operation	Ongoing information system costs can be higher because the systems are generally customized Cash accounting systems generally require more personnel to operate them. However, fewer qualified accountants are necessary	Ongoing operation of systems is more sustainable because (i) it is easier to attract and retain skilled staff; and (ii) subsidiary records are integrated (e.g., payables, receivables and asset registers)

Appendix 3 presents a cost-benefit analysis of New Zealand's implementation of accrual accounting. Based on conservative assumptions, and excluding most benefits, the analysis calculates an internal rate of return (IRR) of +7% for the implementation.

In summary, evidence suggests that:

- At the aggregate level, accrual-based fiscal indicators provide better information about the sustainability of fiscal policies (for instance, the effects of pension policies on a government's balance sheet are disclosed) and provide a stronger basis for government accountability (accrual accounting information can not be manipulated as easily as cash-based information). Furthermore, accrual-based fiscal indicators arguably provide a better measure of the effects of government policies on aggregate demand; and

- At the organization level, accrual-based financial statements provide better measures of organizational efficiency and effectiveness. Accrual-based financial information also reduces opportunities for fraud and corruption, particularly as regards stewardship of assets.

This part reviewed accrual budgeting and accounting from a developed country-perspective. In a DMC setting, the identified benefits might not be realized, because of, for instance, implementation constraints.

IV. DMC Government Accounting

1. Introduction

This part reviews the accounting arrangements of nine DMC governments. All have either (i) announced an intention to move to accrual accounting; (ii) begun implementation activities; or (iii) already adopted modified accrual accounting.

Historical accounting practices influence country accounting arrangements and trends. Based on the Table 4 model categorization, the DMCs are classified into two groups: (i) DMCs using standards-based accounting models; and (ii) DMCs with Soviet accounting backgrounds.[44]

Table 4. Economies Classified by Accounting Models

Accounting System	Accounting Model	Features	Economies
Standards Based Accounting	British Commonwealth	• Commercially driven • Overriding rule is that financial statements show a "fair" picture • Accounting practices reflect, and develop with, business practices • Professional regulation dominates	Australia, Bahamas, Ireland, Fiji Islands, India, Jamaica, Kenya, Malaysia, Netherlands, New Zealand, Pakistan, Papua New Guinea, Zimbabwe, Singapore, South Africa, Sri Lanka, Trinidad & Tobago, United Kingdom
	United States	• Same as British Commonwealth model except that professional regulation coexists with government regulation	Canada, Indonesia, Japan Marshall Islands, Mexico Panama, Philippines, United States

---

[44] Although this classification is for private sector accounting models, it is broadly consistent with government accounting classifications See, for instance, OECD. 2002. Models of Public Budgeting and Accounting Reform. *OECD Journal on Budgeting*. Vol 2(1). December. pp. 5–6.

Accounting System	Accounting Model	Features	Economies
Uniform Accounting Plans	Soviet Union	• Government driven • Dominated by statistics and taxation requirements • Accounting practices are statute-based • Accountancy profession not required	Azerbaijan, People's Republic of China, Mongolia, Russia, Uzbekistan
	Continental European	• Government driven • Dominated by taxation requirements • Accounting practices are statute-based	Belgium, Cambodia, France, Germany, Italy, Spain, Sweden, Switzerland, Viet Nam, Venezuela
	Latin American "Castilian model"	• Very similar to continental European model	Argentina, Bolivia, Chile, Colombia, Ethiopia, Paraguay, Peru, Uruguay

Source: Modified from Nobes, Christopher and Robert Parker. 1995. *Comparative International Accounting*: Fourth Edition: Prentice Hall. p. 67.

2. Standards-Based Accounting Countries

Economies with standards-based accounting backgrounds tend to use cash accounting in government, generally reflecting colonial influences. This section describes government accounting in the Fiji Islands, Indonesia, Marshall Islands, Philippines and Sri Lanka.

Fiji Islands

The financial statements of private sector organizations, government commercial companies and commercial statutory authorities are prepared using the accrual accounting basis. The financial statements of core ministries and departments are prepared using a cash accounting basis in accordance with the *Finance Instructions and Regulations*. However, the Government has purchased a sophisticated accrual-based computer system and has signaled a medium-term intention to move to the accrual accounting basis.[45]

---

[45] ADB. 2002. *Diagnostic Study of Accounting and Auditing Practices in the Fiji Islands*. Manila. p. 80.

The Government's *Finance Instructions* and *Regulations* govern the preparation of cash-based reports, but these instructions are not accounting standards and are not internationally comparable. However, a recent study investigated preferences as to who should set accounting standards for, and monitor their application in, the public sector. Among other things, the study concluded that there is substantial stakeholder support for the introduction of accrual public sector accounting standards within the Fiji Islands.[46]

Indonesia

The State Financial Accounting Agency is responsible for government accounting arrangements. In the absence of public sector accounting standards, financial report preparation was, until very recently, largely based on a 1925 treasury law and private sector accounting standards, some of which are not suitable for public sector reporting.

Work is currently underway to implement GFS in the central Government. In an effort to provide legislative support for public sector financial management reforms, government submitted three bills to parliament in September 2000 (covering state finances, state treasury, and state audit). The State Finance Law was approved on 6 March 2003 and is awaiting Presidential assent. Among other things, this law: (i) requires preparation of central and local government balance sheets and budget realization reports; and (ii) provides a basis for accounting standard-setting arrangements and procedures.

The Government Accounting Standards Committee prepared a seven-year action plan starting in July 2002. The action plan envisages a transition from cash accounting to accrual accounting, culminating with IPSAS-compliant government accounting standards in 2009. The Committee has already prepared 4 IPSAS-based government financial accounting standards (PSAPs).

Marshall Islands

The Marshall Islands follows US government accounting practices as promulgated by the Government Accounting Standards Board (GASB). In particular, section 104 of the *Financial Management Act 1990* requires public sector organizations to account in accordance with GASB

---

[46] Vatuloka, Eroni and Greg E. Shailer. 2000. Preferences for the Regulation and Monitoring of Fijian Government Accounting. *Asian Accounting Review*. Vol(8). No. 2.

standards. Most government accounting is on a modified accrual basis; however, GASB 34 (*Basic Financial Statements—and Management's Discussion and Analysis—for State and Local Governments*) requires a move towards full accrual accounting.[47]

The effective date of GASB 34 requirements depends on total annual government revenues in the first financial year ending after 15 June 1999—in the year ended 30 September 1999 the Government reported revenues of $90.4 million.[48] Therefore, government financial statements have to comply with GASB 34 requirements starting with the financial year beginning on 1 October 2002.

Private sector organizations, state-owned enterprises and statutory authorities use the accrual accounting basis and are required to prepare financial statements in accordance with US GAAP.

Philippines

Fund, obligation and cash-disbursement-ceiling accounting methods are used in government. Taxes are accounted for on the cash basis and the accrual basis is used for other revenues and expenses.[49] Government financial reports and statements, like commercial entities, are prepared based on official accounting records. In the case of government organizations, specific laws and regulations tightly prescribe the format and contents.

The requirement to prepare and submit balance sheets and operating statements was introduced in 1979. Financial statements include (i) current assets, (ii) contingent assets, (iii) fixed assets, (iv) current liabilities, (v) contingent liabilities, (vi) allotted appropriations, (vii) income, (viii) invested surplus, (ix) contingent surplus, (x) national clearing account, (xi) the total surplus, and (xii) assorted notes to the accounts.[50]

---

[47] ADB. 2002. *Diagnostic Study of Accounting and Auditing Practices in the Republic of the Marshall Islands*. Manila. pp. 23-24, 64-65.
[48] Government of the Marshall Islands. 2001. *Republic of the Marshall Islands: General Purpose Financial Statements and Independent Auditors' Report for the year ended 30 September 2000*. Majuro. 18 May. p. 5.
[49] Pobre, Hermogenes P. and Araceli Bernal-Magno. 1987. *Government Accounting*. Manila. pp. 19-21, 307-330.
[50] *Ibid*. pp. 14-15.

The Commission on Audit is planning a move to full accrual accounting. To this end, it is considering the appropriateness of IPSAS as the basis for government accounting standards.

Sri Lanka

The financial statements of private and public sector organizations that are classified as specified business enterprises are prepared using the accrual accounting basis. The budgets and financial statements of other government bodies are prepared using a cash accounting basis.[51]

The Government is considering introducing accrual budgeting and accounting as part of the ADB-supported Public Expenditure Management Reform Program.[52]

3. Soviet Accounting System Countries

The "Soviet accounting system" catered to the needs of central planning; in particular, the system provided accounting information, including (i) financial information, (ii) tax information, and (iii) statistical information. It emphasized standardization and uniformity so that information could be compared across sectors and industries.

The system did not use market-based accounting concepts such as going concern, consistency and substance over form. Furthermore, provisions for doubtful debts or obsolete inventories were not estimated—doubtful accounts were written off only when they were clearly not collectable. Accounting consisted of adhering to prescribed charts of accounts (Uniform Accounting Systems, UAS) that were designed to meet the requirements of the central planning system. The primary function of accounting was to record the factual data necessary to assess plan accomplishments, rather than to assess an organization's financial situation.

Public and "private sector" organizations used the system, which employs double-entry bookkeeping and reflects many aspects of accrual accounting.

---

[51] Government of Sri Lanka. 1992. *Financial Regulations of the Government of the Democratic Socialist Republic of Sri Lanka*. Department of Government Printing: Colombo.
[52] ADB. 2002. *Diagnostic Study of Accounting and Auditing Practices in Sri Lanka*. Manila. pp. 24, 63-64.

Azerbaijan

Government activities are generally accounted for on an accrual accounting basis at the organizational level and on a cash basis for consolidated budgeting and reporting—the cash basis was introduced with support from international institutions, particularly the IMF and the World Bank.

Government organizations prepare monthly cash reports and quarterly accrual reports that are submitted to the MOF. In 2001, the MOF began publishing consolidated quarterly reports incorporating revenues, expenditures, expenditure arrears, stock of government and government-guaranteed debts, and new loans contracted or loan guarantees issued. A revised Budget Systems Law has been drafted and is being considered.[53]

People's Republic of China

With the exception of government organizations, all organizations use double-entry bookkeeping and all transactions are recorded on the accrual basis. Not-for-profit organizations (e.g., schools, kindergartens, hospitals) have recently moved from cash accounting to a modified accrual accounting basis.[54]

Government budget accounting system reform began in 1998. It took account of the PRC's successful enterprise accounting reforms and international public sector accounting practices. Among other things, as a consequence of the initial reforms: (i) the cash accounting basis is required to be used in general budget accounting; (ii) administrative units may use either the cash or accrual basis, depending on their specific circumstances; (iii) double entry bookkeeping has been implemented; (iv) the previous focus on fund sources, applications and balances has been replaced by new accounting elements comprising assets, liabilities, net assets, revenues and expenditures. For example, the Change in Fund Activity Statement became a statement of assets and liabilities, and various statements about financial flows were added.[55]

---

[53] ADB. 2002. *Diagnostic Study of Accounting and Auditing Practices in Azerbaijan.* Manila. p. 50.
[54] ADB. 2000. *Financial Management and Governance Issues in the People's Republic of China.* Manila. p. 8.
[55] Jiwei, Lou (First Vice Minister, Ministry of Finance). 2002. Government Budgeting and Accounting Reform in China. *OECD Journal on Budgeting.* Vol 2(1). December. pp. 51–80.

The adoption of the accrual basis for general budget accounting is now being considered. In particular, accounting principles used in enterprise accounting systems may be gradually introduced. To this end, clear requirements are needed for fixed asset depreciation, overseas investment, income tax and other issues related to their economic activities.[56]

For national accounts purposes (SNA 1993), a national balance sheet has been prepared annually since 1997, but is incomplete and has not yet been published. The biggest issue is valuing non-financial assets.[57]

Mongolia

State-owned enterprises and the central bank are required to prepare IAS-compliant financial statements. Government organizations use modified accrual accounting (revenues are rarely accrued due to budget financing arrangements). Aggregate government reporting is on a cash basis.[58]

Government organizations prepare and submit two major financial statements to the MOF on a quarterly and annual basis: balance sheets and associated notes, and budget performance reports. The contents and formats of these financial statements do not meet IAS or IPSAS requirements. Moreover, non-financial assets (e.g., inventories and physical assets) and some expenses (e.g., utilities) of government organizations are commonly reflected in the financial statements of other entities (e.g., the inventories, physical assets, and utility expenses of the MOF are reported in the financial statements of "Building No. 5"). This issue of entity-definition limits the ability of financial statements to reflect entities' position and performance.[59]

Uzbekistan

Uzbekistan uses sector-neutral accounting. That is, with few exceptions, accounting standards, regulations and procedures apply equally to public sector organizations and to private sector organizations. Budget organizations account and report in accordance with the *Accounting Law*

---

[56] Ibid.
[57] Lihua, Dong (National Bureau of Statistics). 2001. *The Status of Implementation of the 1993 SNA in China*. Paper presented at the concluding workshop on ADB TA No. 5874-REG: Rebasing and Linking of NAS. 13-16 February. p. 3.
[58] ADB. 2000. *Financial Management and Governance Issues in Mongolia*. Manila. p. 47.
[59] Public Sector Performance (NZ) Ltd. April 1999. *Final Report on TA No. 2931-MON: Program Preparation for Governance Reforms: Status Assessment of Pilot Agencies*. Vol III(3). p. 16.

1996, national accounting standards (NAS), Accounting Instructions for Budget Organizations and operational classifications of revenues and expenditures of the State Budget. NAS are being made IAS-compliant.[60]

The *Accounting Law 1996*—which applies to private and public sector organizations—states that the basic accounting principles are the maintenance of accounting records on the basis of the double-entry system; going concern; monetary measurement of transactions, assets and liabilities; reliability; accrual measurement; prudence (conservatism); substance over form; comparability; neutrality; matching principle; and historic cost.[61]

4. Conclusion

This part revealed a general trend among ADB DMCs toward accrual accounting. It also illustrated that there are significant differences between individual countries (see Table 5).

Table 5. Selected ADB DMCs: Direction of Government Accounting

DMC	Current Basis	General Direction
Fiji Islands	Modified cash	Accrual
Indonesia	Modified cash	Accrual
Marshall Islands	Modified cash	Accrual
Philippines	Modified accrual	Accrual
Sri Lanka	Modified cash	Accrual
Azerbaijan	Accrual	Accrual
China, People's Republic of	Modified accrual	Accrual
Mongolia	Modified accrual	Accrual
Uzbekistan	Accrual	Accrual

The review identifies the comparatively advanced accounting methods of economies that formerly used the Soviet accounting system. Nevertheless, the descriptions in this part should be treated carefully for the following reasons that are discussed later in this report:

---

[60] ADB. 2000. *Financial Management and Governance Issues in Uzbekistan.* Manila. p. 22.
[61] *Ibid.*

- Accounting capacity was not considered. For instance, the Marshall Islands is required to introduce accrual accounting, but has no professionally-qualified accountants.

- Government accounting arrangements must be considered in a wider public management context. There may be higher priorities than adopting accrual accounting. For instance, Indonesia is working to reestablish basic accountability following decentralization of government functions.

- Implementation effectiveness was not considered—there are significant differences between regulatory requirements and actual practice. For instance, although Mongolian government accounting appears reasonably advanced, there are significant basic issues (e.g., misleading asset valuations).

- Institutional and environmental rigidities were ignored. For instance, in attempting to improve government accounting arrangements, the Philippines will have to overcome significant resistance from groups with vested interests.

V. Country Implementation Experiences

1. Introduction

A number of developed countries have implemented accrual budgeting and accounting (see Table 2, page 12). This part reviews implementation approaches and experiences. It begins by identifying general implementation tasks then examines the implementation approach taken by New Zealand (NZ), which was chosen because it was the first OECD country to fully implement accrual budgeting and accounting in government—a substantial collection of materials on its experiences have been compiled in the ensuing period.[62] The experiences of four other developed countries are also considered in order to identify implementation approaches and lessons (see Appendix 4).

2. General Implementation Tasks

A variety of strategies, sequences and timeframes may apply to adopting accrual accounting. Nevertheless, the following **preparatory activities** will generally be required, once a decision has been taken to adopt accrual accounting:

- Reviewing existing systems, arrangements and capacity;
- Developing an implementation strategy and project plan;
- Developing a communication/education strategy;
- Developing a training/capacity enhancement strategy and plan;
- Establishing project teams;
- Agreeing to accounting policies and reporting formats;
- Identifying accounting information system requirements;
- Clarifying external and internal audit roles; and
- Designing quality assurance processes.

---

[62] Although Iceland implemented accrual budgeting and accounting at around the same time as NZ, little has been written on its experiences. Moreover, it should be recognized that governments using the Soviet accounting system introduced accrual accounting concepts many decades before NZ.

Implementation activities will generally include

- Developing charts of account and detailed accounting policies and instructions;
- Delivering communication and training programs;
- Establishing opening balance sheets (identifying and valuing assets and liabilities);
- Implementing changes to information systems, where necessary;
- Auditing opening balance sheets; and
- Implementing changed internal control and audit arrangements.

3. The New Zealand Experience

In the mid-1980s, NZ began a decade-long process of rigorous reforms including exchange rate liberalization, labor-market deregulation, privatization and public sector management reform. As part of the public sector reforms, government budgeting and reporting moved from the cash to the accrual basis over about a 6-year period (see Table 6).

Table 6. Implementing Accrual Budgeting and Accounting in New Zealand

Year	Event
1987	Departments begin preparations for accrual accounting
1989	Public Finance Act passed
	Departments begin move to accrual accounting (first five go live) (July)
1990	All departments except three on accrual accounting (June)
	Final departments go live (December)
1991	First half-year whole-of-government financial statements (December)
1992	First annual whole-of-government financial statements (June)
	First half-year consolidated whole-of-government financial statements (December)
1993	First annual consolidated whole-of-government financial statements (June)
1994	First consolidated accrual budget (June)
	First monthly consolidated whole-of-government financial statements (October)
2002	First fully line-by-line consolidated whole-of-government financial statements

Source: Updated from Warren, Ken. 2000. The Impact of GAAP on Fiscal Decision Making: A Review of Ten Years Experience with accrual and output-based budgets in New Zealand. Paper prepared for the Australasian Treasury Officers Conference. October. Modifications and additions have been made.[63]

Objectives and Effectiveness

The initial objective of the NZ public sector reforms was to enhance technical efficiency and improve accountability (see, for instance, the Public Finance Act 1989, State-Owned Enterprises Act 1986, and the State Sector Act 1988). This emphasis was later extended to achieving aggregate fiscal discipline. Figure 3 reveals a marked improvement in NZ fiscal aggregates, some of which was due to the introduction of accrual-based budgeting and reporting (but the precise impacts cannot be quantified). The overall reforms are credited with improving fiscal control, efficiency, asset management and public sector culture (see Figure 3).

First, a 1997 study contended that the relative slackness of the NZ system, with respect to aggregate fiscal discipline, declined from 74% in 1984 to 6% in 1994.[64] The authors opined that "prior to the reforms, most public financial statements and budgetary documents were not available to the general public for scrutiny and, even if they were made available, they could not be easily understood even by accountants and financial experts in the private sector. Consequently, government performance was largely non-transparent. The [adoption of accrual accounting] changed this dramatically." (p. 432).

---

[63] The coauthor of this report was the Coordinator of Aggregate Fiscal Forecasting and Monitoring at the NZ Treasury when the Government moved its aggregate budgets and reports from the cash to the accrual basis. In this role, he was responsible for coordinating, preparing and analyzing the Government's forecasts, budgets and financial reports (cash based, accrual based, SNA and GFS). He was also responsible for implementing and maintaining the Government's financial information system. During the early part of the reform process, when accrual accounting was introduced at the organizational level, he was involved in audits of public sector departments and state-owned enterprises, while at the Audit Office.

[64] Campos, J. E., & Pradhan, S. 1997. Evaluating public expenditure management systems: An experimental methodology with an application to the Australia and New Zealand reforms. *Journal of Policy Analysis and Management*, 16(3), 423-445.

"...for the first time, it was possible to apply these accounting concepts and disciplines to the budget process and fiscal management. The Government's determination to apply sustained fiscal discipline was hugely aided by the availability of such sophisticated and effective accounting tools. The Budget of 1991 yielded a huge fiscal dividend extracted from the application of these modern tools. The credibility of our fiscal policy framework was further boosted by the requirement that all this accounting and budgeting had to be conducted in compliance with generally accepted accounting practice. Maintenance and enforcement of those accounting standards is entrusted to a private entity independent of the Government. In this way a government, were it to be so tempted, is denied the ability to engage in self-serving interpretations."

— Former NZ Finance Minister, Ruth Richardson[65]

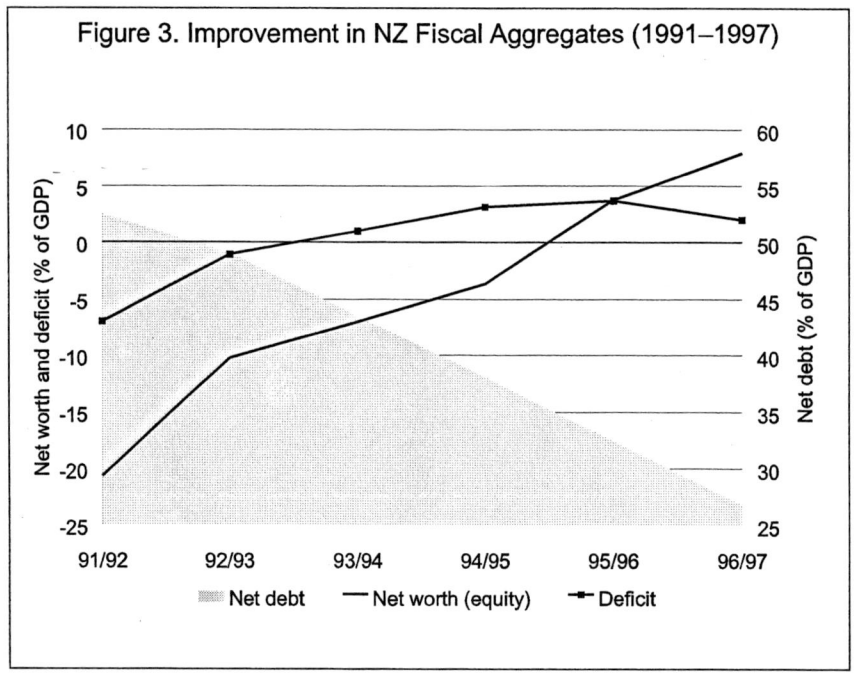

Source: New Zealand Treasury.

---

[65] Richardson, Ruth. Opening and Balancing the Books: The New Zealand Experience in IFAC. 1996. *Perspectives on Accrual Accounting*. Occasional Paper 3. New York: Public Sector Committee. p. 9.

By using independently-determined accounting rules (GAAP) for its fiscal forecasts and results, the Government was able to demonstrate its commitment to transparent budgeting. Any government faces difficulty in demonstrating commitment to prudent fiscal management when it sets the rules on how it accounts for its results. The independence of the GAAP standard-setting process from government allowed this difficulty to be addressed. The presentation and format of the financial statements was also familiar to those with a general knowledge of accounting. As a result, debates on fiscal results shifted to matters of economic substance rather than on the appropriate accounting form.[66]

Second, evidence on the impact of the reforms, in terms of decision making and efficiency, comes from a number of sources. For instance, a 1996 study provided evidence of efficiency gains, measured in terms of the unit cost of outputs.[67]

Third, anecdotal evidence indicates that in the past decade, the public sector culture has shifted to that of a managerial culture with a service orientation.[68] This was supported by professionalization of the government accounting and auditing cadre.

Fourth, the adoption of accrual accounting was the "unqualified success story" of the reform process. In a survey of the broad range of public sector management reforms, a "scorecard" was produced—accrual reforms received the highest grade among government managers.[69]

NZ public sector arrangements have been criticized for excessive emphasis on contracting (e.g., the use of performance agreements between ministers and department heads)[70] and an explicit emphasis on efficiency over equity (e.g., there was a significant reduction in public

---

[66] Warren, Ken. 2000. The Impact of GAAP on Fiscal Decision Making: A Review of Ten Years Experience with accrual and output-based budgets in New Zealand. Paper prepared for the Australasian Treasury Officers Conference. October.

[67] Brumby, J., Edmonds, P., & Honeyfield, K. 1996. Effects of public sector financial management reform in New Zealand. Paper presented at the Australasian Evaluation Society Conference, Wellington, New Zealand, 30 August.

[68] Schick, A. 1996. *The Spirit of Reform: Managing the New Zealand State Sector in a Time of Change*, Wellington, New Zealand: State Services Commission.

[69] Stace, D. & Norman, R. 1995. *Re-invented Government: The New Zealand Experience.* Centre for Corporate Change, Australian Graduate School of Management, University of New South Wales, CCC Paper No. 050.

[70] Boston, J. (ed.). 1995. *The State Under Contract.* Wellington, New Zealand: Bridget Williams Books.

sector employment).[71] Indeed, some commentators have warned developing countries about adopting aspects of the NZ public model—particularly devolving authority to managers.[72] Nevertheless, NZ's experience has influenced other countries such as Canada[73] and the US:

> "When President Clinton and I began what we call Reinventing Government ... we borrowed a great deal from other nations—such as the establishment of government-wide financial standards—personally recommended to me by New Zealand's Treasury Secretary, Graham Scott." — Former US Vice President Albert Gore[74]

Implementation Approach

NZ—in common with other countries such as Australia and the US—made government organizations responsible for implementing accrual budgeting and accounting. The Treasury (Finance Ministry) coordinated an education and communication campaign involving booklets, a video, journal, magazine and newspaper articles and many conferences, seminars and presentations. A central Financial Management Assurance function within Treasury provided a strategic internal audit role, and a consultancy service to departments during migration. Minimal training was provided to departments.[75]

Departments individually received approval to move onto the new system. The enabling legislation—the Public Finance Act 1989—provided strong incentives for them to meet implementation benchmarks. It gave departments 2 years to develop their own accrual-based

---

[71] Kelsey, J. 1995. *The New Zealand Experiment: A World Model for Structural Adjustment?* Auckland University Press/Bridget Williams Books.

[72] Schick, A. 1998. Why Most Developing Countries Should Not Try New Zealand's Reforms. *World Bank Research Observer* (February).

[73] See for instance:
- Schwartz, H. M. 1997. Reinvention and retrenchment: Lessons from the application of the New Zealand model to Alberta, Canada, *Journal of Policy Analysis and Management*, 16(3), 405-421.
- Canadian Office of the Auditor General. 1995. *Toward Better Governance: Public Service Reform in New Zealand (1984-1994) and its Relevance to Canada.* Ottawa, Canada: Minister of Supply and Services.

[74] Gore, Albert. 1999. Remarks delivered at the Opening Session of the International REGO Conference. 14 January.

[75] IFAC Public Sector Committee. 1994. *Implementing Accrual Accounting in Government: The New Zealand Experience.* Occasional Paper 1. October. New York.

systems, but this was achieved by most in a year and by all within 18 months.[76]

Specific NZ Implementation Issues and Lessons

This section describes selected NZ implementation issues and lessons.[77]

Personnel skills and numbers. Few government finance functions grew in terms of personnel numbers. There was however a significant upgrading in financial expertise as compliance officers were replaced with professional staff capable of negotiating budgets and marketing financial information. The Treasury was able to make reductions in staff responsible for routine accounting functions, from 6 regional offices, employing about 50 personnel, to 6 staff.

Training and capacity building. The Treasury did not provide training for departmental financial managers. This was in opposition to strong views that training was necessary to realize the benefits and reduce the risks associated with the new regime. In keeping with the wider reforms, the approach was intended to promote self-reliance among departments. In hindsight, it was the right decision.

Computerized accounting systems. An advantage of accrual accounting systems was that activities—such as commitments or purchase order systems, payroll, fixed assets, creditors and debtors—were integrated into one system. This reduced double processing and reconciliation problems, and resulted in significant time savings.

The central accounting system was modularized into individual accounting systems. This assisted departmental flexibility, by ensuring that accounting systems can keep pace with technology and can continue to meet changing needs, as departmental activities change—one department can take advantage of new system features of particular value to its organization without having to refer to the rest of the bureaucracy.

Several departments initially implemented accounting systems where significant authority (for example to add ledger codes) was given

---

[76] *Ibid.*

[77] This section is directly based on the following paper prepared by Ken Warren of the NZ Treasury: IFAC Public Sector Committee. 1994. *Implementing Accrual Accounting in Government: The New Zealand Experience.* Occasional Paper 1. October. New York.

to regional offices. These were quickly found to be cumbersome and were hurriedly recentralized.

Property (land) valuations. Departments and auditors found it particularly difficult to ensure that all properties were reported. It was necessary to coordinate searches of government valuation records with the Land Transfer Office and individual departments—previous asset records were found to be of little value and significant resources were required to identify all the property holdings and obtain auditable valuations. This work however had a most valuable spin-off in identifying surplus properties that could be sold.

Reliability of information. Assurance over the reliability of the information was derived from three sources. First, departmental chief executives and chief financial officers were required to sign a statement of responsibility with the consolidation schedules that to the best of their knowledge they were a fair reflection of their financial results. Second, the Financial Management Assurance team reviewed the consolidation schedules and draft financial statements with the resulting analysis providing some measure of comfort. Third, the full audit carried out by the Audit Office provided assurance through the opinion attached to the financial statements.

Demand for information. Unless decision makers demand and use accrual information, then the implementation is less likely to succeed. Significant efforts were made to educate ministers, parliamentarians and the media about uses for accrual-based information. This helped create demand.

Costs of implementing accrual accounting. The costs of implementing accrual accounting systems compared with cash systems were relatively trivial. Overly centralized accounting processes—with poorly-integrated subsidiary elements—are cumbersome and expensive compared to private sector practices of centralized cash management and streamlined financial management systems.

Leveraging off private sector accounting. Major gains were achieved by leveraging off private sector accounting. By making use of GAAP the best of private sector off-the-shelf accounting software could be used and the pool of skills and expertise available to the financial management reform was sufficiently widened to cope with the new demands and make benefit from the new opportunities.

Better information doesn't necessarily change results. Accrual information provides a better basis for budgetary decision-making. It also widened the issues that are considered. However, the objectives of the decisions did not change. Furthermore, the improved results—for example reduced debt and unit output prices—were facilitated rather than caused by the accounting system. Indeed, the fiscal improvements achieved by government were primarily due to political will. A less sophisticated system could have achieved a great deal in the presence of that political will, and an even more sophisticated system would achieve very little if the political will to use it were not present.[78]

Only so much can be achieved immediately. Change is resource intensive. In the early years of accrual budgeting, the main pressure on change was in achieving a set of budget documentation that provided the information. Only when this was in place were we in a position to concentrate our resources on streamlining the processes. The automated-checking processes now used to collect and collate financial information were simply not possible until the basic structures were in place (see Box 8).

4. Implementation Issues and Lessons

The implementation experiences reviewed in the preceding sections, together with other country experiences (see Appendix 4),[79] and a recent OECD paper[80] provide a basis for identifying general implementation issues and lessons.

---

[78] Warren, Ken. 2000. *The Impact of GAAP on Fiscal Decision Making: A Review of Ten Years Experience with accrual and output-based budgets in New Zealand.* Paper prepared for the Australasian Treasury Officers Conference. October.

[79] See, for example:
- IFAC. 2003. *The Modernization of Government Accounting in France: The Current Situation, the Issues and the Outlook.* New York. Public Sector Committee.
- OECD. 1997. Iceland's budget and financial accounting reform. http://www1.oecd.org/puma/focus/compend/is.htm#Iceland's%20budget%20and%20financial%20accounting%20reform [accessed on 12 December 2002].

[80] OECD. 2002. *Accrual Accounting and Budgeting: Key Issues and Recent Developments.* Paris.

Box 8. Process Automation

The New Zealand Government went through a variety of approaches to consolidating and preparing accrual reports and budgets. Several interim steps were taken. This enabled processes to mature and requirements to be better understood:

- Departmental financial statements (cash and accrual) were initially collected by spreadsheets and uploaded into (i) a simple commercial general ledger, for preparation of cash and accrual reports; and (ii) a purpose-built database, for preparation and analysis of budgets. The information was then reentered into spreadsheets for final consolidation. This approach had minimal cost and worked, but presented significant problems:
    - Departmental financial forecasts and reports were often internally inconsistent (e.g., balance sheets did not balance and cash flow statements were inconsistent with other financial statements)
    - The collection spreadsheets were error-prone as was the database. Moreover, the process entailed management of hundreds of computer diskettes; and
    - It took weeks for reports and budgets to be collected, reviewed, amended, consolidated, analyzed and published.
- An integrated financial consolidation system was procured and implemented in 1994 (for a cost of about $700,000, including implementation support, hardware and software). The system
    - Introduced automated validation tests. These tests (of which there were over 1,000) ensured that clean data was provided to Treasury;
    - Automated data collection and consolidation (information was transmitted via modem);
    - Amalgamated forecast, budget and actual data into one system; and
    - Supported advanced analysis.
- The following benefits were achieved:
    - Accurate data was provided within 10 working days of month-end;
    - Consolidations could then be performed instantly;
    - Significant reductions in personnel numbers were achieved;
    - Other resources were freed from basic accounting and redirected towards analysis; and
    - Consolidated government financial statements could be published within 4 weeks of month-end.
- A final step was taken in 1997-2000, when the system was rebuilt as an Internet-based database.

Quality assurance is important

A quality assurance procedure is desirable and implementation benchmarks should be included in the implementation strategy as an incentive mechanism. This can create a sense of competition among entities.

Communications are essential

The countries that first moved to accruals generally cite the need for more and better communications as the single biggest factor that was underestimated during implementation.[81]

Close communication with the supreme audit institution (SAI) is essential. The SAI should reinforce the reform process and assist entities in implementation.

Communicating with politicians—notably parliamentarians—is an ongoing challenge for most countries that have introduced accruals. First, initial support from politicians may decline with successive elections when new politicians are not adequately communicated with. Second, in most countries, a small group of ministers and legislature members have taken the decision to adopt accruals. But, when accrual information starts arriving, it has confused other politicians as very little effort was made to communicate with them. This potentially undermines the legislature's ability to effectively hold the executive to account. The lesson is to have a strong communication strategy when accrual accounting is being introduced and to maintain it over time.

Experience also reveals a communications gap with the media and, by extension, with the public. There can be confusion when accrual budgets and financial statements are first introduced. In particular, the media may have limited understanding of the figures and the underlying concepts. Some countries have successfully combated this risk through media training sessions, and by having experts available in the media "lock-up room" when the budget is introduced.

The number and mix of accounting personnel will change

Suitably-qualified accountants need to be employed and cash-trained government accountants need to be reeducated. Where a country has an absolute shortage of accounting skills, this needs to be considered when implementation strategies and schedules are designed. However, it is

---

[81] OECD. 2002. *Accrual Accounting and Budgeting: Key Issues and Recent Developments*. Paris.

important not to over-invest in training—some countries have overestimated the need for training. Consideration should be given as to how surplus accounting staff are to be handled.

Use commercially-available financial management information systems

New financial management information system (FMIS) implementations often accompany the introduction of accruals. A very clear lesson is for governments to opt for commercial software and to adjust internal processes where necessary. Problems occur—and costs rise—when governments build their own systems or make significant modifications to commercial software.

Many FMISs are replaced within a short period of their implementation (almost all departmental FMISs used in NZ were replaced after just 2 years). This reflects poor decisions being made about organizational needs, because managers are unfamiliar with their information needs under accrual accounting. The lesson is not to invest in a complex FMIS, until the organization has familiarized itself with the accrual environment.

Encourage improved information quality and timeliness

There are often problems with the timeliness and accuracy of submissions to the finance ministry. Some countries have achieved significant improvements in information quality and submission dates, by keeping league tables of when the various accounting units submit this information and the number of adjustments that have to be made. This lesson is true both of cash and accrual information.

Have guidance and accounting policies ready early

Countries that have already implemented accrual budgeting and accounting have produced a wide range of guidance and training materials. It is essential to have the specific new accounting policies available early so that line ministries and agencies can prepare for them from the earliest possible moment. The use of task forces on specific issues composed of officials from a range of ministries and agencies serves to get buy-in from them more readily than otherwise.

Commitment accounting provides a good starting point

Many countries, both developing and developed, use a form of commitment accounting. This involves reporting committing resources, even though cash may not have been paid. Commitment accounting—as for instance, used in the Philippines—has many similarities to accrual accounting and can provide a good starting point for introducing accrual-based accounting.

Budgeting and reporting basis should be consistent

The problem with applying accruals only to financial reporting and not to the budget is that accrual information may not be taken seriously. The budget is the key management document in the public sector and accountability is based on implementing the budget as approved by the legislature. If the budget is on cash basis, that is going to be the dominant basis on which politicians and senior civil servants work. Financial reporting on a different basis, risks becoming a purely technical accounting exercise in these cases. To maximize benefits, countries must fully implement accrual budgeting and accounting.

Furthermore, even though budgets and reports may be prepared on the accrual basis, different accounting frameworks may be applied. This causes complexity and confusion. For instance, budgets for the Australian budget sector are prepared on the GFS basis. Financial reports are prepared in accordance with Australian accounting standards. The operating balance measure produced by these two accounting frameworks can differ quite significantly, with non-trivial implications for fiscal policy.[82]

5. Conclusion

This part reviewed implementation experiences and identified several lessons. Most importantly, there is no first-best implementation approach. Rather, this will depend on country arrangements and circumstances.

Perhaps the overriding lesson is that implementing accruals cannot be seen as a technical accounting exercise. It needs to involve a

---

[82] Robinson, Marc. 2001. The Treatment of Revaluations in Accrual-Based Government Accounts. *Journal of Accounting, Accountability and Performance*. Vol 7(2).

"culture change" in government and be linked with wider public management reforms. For accruals to be worthwhile and successful, the new information that accruals brings forth needs to be used to improve decision-making in government. This change will not necessarily happen automatically. It needs to be actively promoted, especially at the level of policy makers and senior officials.[83] A recent IMF working paper considers this issue further (see Box 9).

Box 9. Performance Budgeting: Is Accrual Accounting Necessary?

A recent IMF working paper reviews the role of accounting from the perspective of performance budgeting reforms.[84] The paper argues that, while many OECD countries have moved their accounting systems from a cash to an accrual basis, such a move is perhaps only worthwhile in the context of adopting much wider public sector management reforms. Moreover, while recognizing that accrual accounting does support public management best practices, it argues that many of the objectives of performance-oriented budgeting can be attained by less-than-full accrual accounting, and that unless certain preconditions are met, it is safer for countries to remain with and improve their cash-based accounting systems.

However, the following criticisms might be made of the arguments presented in the paper. First, it overstates the preconditions for moving to an accrual-based system. For instance, it incorrectly assumes that accrual accounting must be introduced together with decentralized accounting and management, thereby weakening basic compliance. Second, the paper disregards evidence regarding the inherent benefits of accrual-based reporting. Third, it strongly advocates supplementing cash-based information with accrual information. While valid as a transitional approach, practical developing and developed country experience reveals that non-integrated ledgers and registers, such as asset registers, quickly become out-of-step with core financial information.

Nevertheless, the paper is consistent with this report in advocating a gradual step-by-step approach to the introduction of accrual accounting.

---

[83] OECD. 2002. *Accrual Accounting and Budgeting: Key Issues and Recent Developments*. Paris.
[84] Diamond, Jack. 2002. *Performance Budgeting: Is Accrual Accounting Required?* Working Paper WP/02/240. Washington, DC: IMF.

VI. Implications and Recommendations for DMCs

1. Introduction

The preceding parts reviewed the advantages and disadvantages of accrual accounting, country implementation experiences and the status of government accounting in selected ADB DMCs. A general trend towards adoption of accrual accounting in government was revealed.

However, the previous parts largely focused on implementation issues in developed country settings. The DMC environment is very different. For instance, there is often a chronic shortage of qualified accounting personnel in the private sector, let alone the public sector. Moreover, DMCs cannot all be grouped together: there are significant differences depending on stage-of-development, historical influences and fiscal pressures, among other things.

Most importantly, DMCs do not have the same latitude as developed countries to make mistakes in allocating scarce government resources. In a developed country, poor financial management may result in unnecessary higher taxes, higher debt or longer waiting times for government-provided services. In a DMC, the implications of poor financial management are much more severe.

This part identifies DMC-specific circumstances that should be considered when accrual budgeting and accounting are being contemplated. It then considers the implementation of accrual accounting in a DMC environment.

2. The DMC Environment is Fundamentally Different

The general DMC environment is more hostile to successful reform

In addition to the government management issues faced by developed countries, most DMCs confront special problems due to extremely constrained resources, inadequate skills and information, pressure to spend more than they can afford on unmet needs, and limited reserves to ride out shocks or unexpected difficulties.

The challenges faced by DMCs are fundamentally different from those of developed countries—the prescriptions and processes that are appropriate for the latter may hold disappointing results in the former. DMCs generally have greater difficulty maintaining fiscal discipline and pursuing efficient budget outcomes. They have weaker control of their budgetary fate, and outcomes that appear to be the result of lax expenditure management often are byproducts of under-development.[85]

Countries transiting from central planning to a market basis (e.g., Uzbekistan) are different too. Many DMCs have small public sectors, but transitional country governments tend to be very large relative to the overall economy. They do not have the option of allowing public management institutions to evolve as the public sector grows, but must replace subsidies with transfers, dismantle state enterprises, establish and administer new tax systems, and forge regulatory institutions that facilitate open, robust markets. The progress made by some transitional countries has been remarkable, but the adjustment of others has been less rapid. However, even the most advanced of the transitional economies still have much unfinished business in managing their finances.

Differences between developed and developing countries both promote and impede reform. On the one hand, developing countries can adopt practices that have evolved over the years and have become widely accepted in the developed world; on the other hand, the special problems facing poor countries may make them inhospitable venues for certain practices.

Capacity constraints can be overwhelming

In comparison to developed countries, DMCs often face extreme capacity constraints: particularly regarding qualified accounting personnel. However, this differs between DMCs. For instance, while the Marshall Islands does not have any qualified accountants in either the public or private sector, Sri Lanka has a large pool of highly qualified private sector accountants.

---

[85] Schick, Allen. 1998. *A Contemporary Approach to Public Expenditure Management.* Washington, DC: World Bank.

Other priorities may be more urgent

In addition to having higher capacity, developed countries tend to face less pressing issues compared to DMCs. For instance, Indonesia is struggling with the loss of accountability due to the massive decentralization program. Diverting effort and resources to accrualization may be unwise in the face of these competing priorities.

Corruption and vested interests can undermine efforts

Extensive efforts have been made in the past 2 decades to improve basic government financial management, including budgeting and accounting, in DMCs. However, most of these efforts have failed, or at least failed to deliver significant improvements, in the face of vested interests or corruption. In particular, attempts to improve government transparency and accountability directly threaten the income sources of politicians and bureaucrats. Given the superior ability of accrual-based accounting to reduce corruptive opportunities, vociferous opposition can be expected to reforms of this nature.

Conflicting donor activities may reduce coherence

Most donors have placed improved public sector governance at the top of their agenda. Consequently, there is a danger that the coherence of reform efforts will be undermined by conflicting methodologies and objectives. In contrast, developed countries do not face this challenge, as they do not generally rely on external support.

Reform fatigue may impede progress

The past decade has seen significant changes in the government arrangements of most DMCs—particularly transition economies. To this end, consideration should be given to the desirability of fundamentally changing financial arrangements.

Limited infrastructure can reduce options

Many DMCs face communication and technological constraints, for instance Internet availability and support for modern FMISs. This reduces choices over FMIS selection.

Supreme audit institutions may lack capacity

Many DMCs have very weak SAIs that are characterized by an absence of professionally-qualified accountants.

3. Seven Key Recommendations for DMC Governments

Accrual accounting implementations will have similar endpoints, because of uniform standards (see pages 7–14). But starting points will vary markedly reflecting country backgrounds, arrangements and practices. Together with other issues, such as country resources and capacity, these factors will determine suitable implementation paths and timing.

Carefully consider implementation strategies

There are two broad implementation models: the big bang approach and the incremental approach.

At one extreme is the **big bang** approach. Typified by NZ, this involved moving all central government entities to full accrual accounting and budgeting in a short period. Accrual financial statements were prepared within 18 months, following which most resources were appropriated on an accrual basis and whole-of-government financial statements and fiscal forecasts were subsequently prepared.

The advantages of the big bang approach include (i) supporting a uniform culture change in government; (ii) achieving quick results; and (iii) avoiding the risk of reversion. Disadvantages include (i) the concentrated workload; (ii) the lack of time to deal with arising issues; and (iii) a danger that political commitment will falter.[86]

The alternative is the **incremental** approach. Implementation timings may vary by organization type and size (for instance, US state entities were classified into three groups, depending on size—each group

---

[86] OECD. 2002. *Accrual Accounting and Budgeting: Key Issues and Recent Developments*. Paris.

has different implementation targets).[87] The incremental approach is taken by most countries and typically involves introducing double-entry bookkeeping, gradually identifying and valuing assets, gradually improved financial reports and finally preparing accrual-based budgets.

The benefits of the incremental approach include: (i) accruals can be pilot tested for several years until finally unveiled, during this time problems can be identified and addressed; (ii) the cash system can be maintained in parallel thereby reducing risks. The disadvantages of the incremental approach include: (i) if government opts to maintain two parallel systems this can be overwhelming in terms of resources and management, however, this can be overcome by gradually altering existing systems (e.g., Sweden); (ii) culture change may not take hold; and (iii) momentum may be lost, especially if implementation takes an extended time.

The big bang approach worked well in NZ's case, but it is important to note that three favorable factors contributed to this success. First, a fiscal crisis gave the reforms momentum. Second, political support was bipartisan and unequivocal. Third, public service employment and procurement reforms gave agencies flexibility over resources. In particular, they were able to recruit accounting personnel readily from the private sector and procure accounting systems. These factors may not be present in other environments (particularly in DMCs), in which case the lower-risk incremental approach may be more appropriate.

A quality assurance procedure is desirable, and implementation benchmarks should be included in the implementation strategy as

---

[87] GASB. 1999 June. *GASB 34 Basic Financial Statements—and Management's Discussion and Analysis—for State and Local Governments*. Washington, DC. Effective Dates:
- Phase 1—Financial statements for periods beginning after 15 June 2001, for governments with total annual revenues of $100 million or more in the first fiscal year ending after 15 June 1999. Different provisions apply for reporting general infrastructure assets at transition.
- Phase 2—Financial statements for periods beginning after 15 June 2002, for governments with total annual revenues of $10 million or more but less than $100 million in the first fiscal year ending after 15 June 1999. Different provisions apply for reporting general infrastructure assets at transition.
- Phase 3—Financial statements for periods beginning after 15 June 2003, for governments with total annual revenues of less than $10 million in the first fiscal year ending after 15 June 1999. Different provisions apply for reporting general infrastructure assets at transition.

an incentive mechanism. In particular, this can create a sense of competition among entities.

Political commitment is essential

If political will is important for financial management reform in developed countries, it is essential in DMCs. In particular, political will is needed to combat vested interests. To this end, it is essential that implementation and communication strategies are designed so that early benefits can be realized. Moreover, implementation strategies should not depend solely on one administration—government changes are frequent in DMCs.

Intentions and objectives must be communicated

Significant emphasis should be placed on communicating the intentions and objectives of the reform process. In comparison to developed countries, a wider group will need to be consulted—a particular effort should be made to gain support from donor organizations.

Suitably qualified accounting personnel are necessary

Suitably qualified accounting personnel will be needed. First, training and recruitment requirements should not be overestimated (see page 50). Second, mechanisms must be designed to either recruit or contract accountants from the private sector. If, as in the case of the Marshall Islands, qualified accountants are not available, consideration should be given to delaying implementation until suitable capacity is present.

Accounting information systems should be appropriate

Attempts are often made to implement accrual accounting on the back of an FMIS implementation. These efforts often fail or involve significant cost or time overruns—particularly when attempts are made to implement complex systems. In the first instance, efforts should be made to supplement existing systems. Moreover, in the DMC setting, it is essential that FMISs can be supported in the country.

Supreme audit institutions must be suitably resourced

The SAI will play a key role in the implementation of accrual accounting. However, the professionalization of an SAI may take many years. For instance, the Fiji Islands and NZ took several years to fully staff their audit offices with qualified accountants.

In the absence of a suitably staffed and resourced SAI, serious consideration should be given to deferring implementation.

The exercise should be part of wider reforms

Implementing accruals cannot be seen as a technical accounting exercise. It needs to involve a "culture change" in government and be linked with wider public management reforms. For accruals to be worthwhile and successful, the new information that accruals brings forth needs to be used to improve government decision-making. This change will not necessarily happen automatically. It needs to be actively promoted, especially at the level of policymakers and senior officials.

4. A Possible Implementation Approach

The inherent constraints of the DMC environment will rarely make the big bang implementation approach suitable. Moreover, while only two accounting bases have an agreed conceptual basis—cash and accrual accounting—from a practical perspective, most government financial statements are prepared on a modified cash or modified accrual basis (see Figure 4).

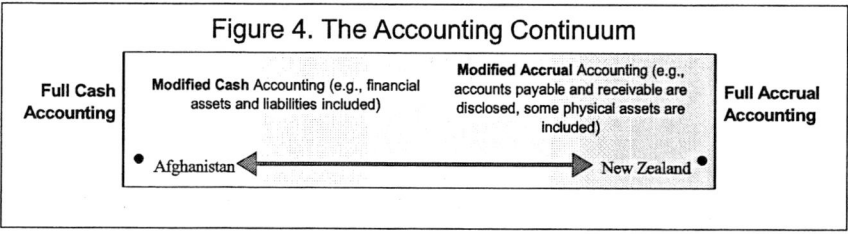

Figure 4. The Accounting Continuum

Nevertheless, most accrual opponents address their objections towards the full accrual accounting basis, without recognizing that benefits can be gained with minimal effort by incorporating additional information in government financial statements. Indeed, the absence of accounting standards does not (and should not) preclude governments from gradually moving to the accrual accounting basis.

The incremental approach involves making progress along the accounting continuum, as capacity and resources allow. In relation to the new accrual-based GFS, the IMF recognizes that implementing the revised system will take some time and will need to progress at a pace determined by the differing needs and circumstances of each country. In particular, many countries will need to revise their underlying accounting systems to reflect the accrual basis of recording and revised classifications.[88] Taken by most countries, the incremental approach can involve the stages outlined in Table 7.

Table 7. An Incremental Approach to Implementing Accrual Accounting

	Step	Effect
1.	Develop a detailed action plan. The plan should consider likely legislative changes. It should also identify communication initiatives.	Will identify potential problems so that they can be addressed in a timely manner. It will also enable resource requirements to be identified.
2.	Implement the cash-based IPSAS. Ensure that cash is recorded on a consistent basis. Most importantly, determine the reporting entity and reconcile all cash balances.	Will address several of the shortcomings of the cash accounting basis
3.	Alter reporting formats. Retain the cash accounting basis, but alter charts of account and reporting formats to reflect accrual principles.	Gives information preparers and users time to familiarize themselves with new reporting formats. It also enables information gaps to be easily identified.
4.	Strengthen SOE accounting. Improve public enterprise accounting and reporting in line with private sector (accrual) accounting standards.	Likely to yield immediate gains through the identification of quasi-fiscal activities and government liabilities
5.	Supplement existing information. Supplement existing accounting information with accounts receivables and payables, thereby introducing basic double-entry bookkeeping and rudimentary accrual accounting.	Provides useful decision-making information on revenue and expense arrears, with minimal additional effort
6.	Identify new asset purchases. Begin categorizing new fixed asset purchases into appropriate expenditure categories (e.g., land, buildings, computer hardware and software).	Provides a sound basis for future identification, classification, valuation and depreciation of fixed assets
7.	Identify contingencies. Identify, value and disclose contingent liabilities and guarantees.	These are usually very important in DMCs. Risk identification is the first stage in risk management.
8.	Identify major assets and liabilities. Identify and value significant assets and liabilities, beginning with financial items and pension obligations.	It is likely that a few major assets and liabilities will comprise most of the balance sheet.

---

[88] IMF. 2001. *Government Finance Statistics Manual*. Washington, DC. paras 1.31–1.33.

Step	Effect
9. Identify other assets. Gradually identify and value other assets, including property and infrastructure assets.	It may take several years for an accurate register of fixed assets to be assembled.
10. Incorporate assets into the financial statements. Incorporate all assets, including fixed assets, into the financial statements and begin expensing depreciation.	Full financial statements are prepared.
11. Prepare accrual budgets and introduce accrual appropriations. Once accrual accounting and reporting is firmly established.	It may take some years until the legislature accepts accrual appropriations, given that a country's appropriation system is constitutionally fundamental.

IPSAS = International Public Sector Accounting Standards; SOE = State-owned enterprise.

5. Conclusion

There is a trend for developed-country adoption of accrual budgeting and accounting. Many DMCs are, or are considering, following suit.

While recognizing the benefits of accrual budgeting and accounting, this report emphasizes the additional constraints and barriers faced by DMCs. In particular, over the past 2 decades, significant efforts have been made to improve basic recordkeeping and cash accounting in DMCs—but these efforts have often failed due to a lack of ongoing commitment, resource constraints, complexity and strong opposition from groups with vested interests. Not surprisingly, some experienced commentators view DMC adoption of accrual budgeting and accounting as unrealistic.

This report concludes that DMCs adopting accrual budgeting and accounting should do so in a realistic and practical manner, as resources and capacity allow. This is why this report supports a step-by-step approach. Most importantly, the process should be incremental, allowing professional capacity (such as in the SAI) to be developed.

To this end, IFAC's recent approval of the cash-based IPSAS provides a sound basis for improving DMC government accounting. Importantly, the IPSAS identifies supplementary accounting disclosures (such as commitments) that can be gradually introduced. By doing so, DMC governments will be able to improve their financial information in a manner consistent with eventual adoption of accrual accounting.

References

ADB. 2002. *Diagnostic Study of Accounting and Auditing Practices in the Fiji Islands*. Manila.

———. 2002. *Diagnostic Study of Accounting and Auditing Practices in the Republic of the Marshall Islands*. Manila.

———. 2002. *Diagnostic Study of Accounting and Auditing Practices in Sri Lanka*. Manila.

———. 2002. *Diagnostic Study of Accounting and Auditing Practices in Azerbaijan*. Manila.

———. 2000. *Financial Management and Governance Issues in Mongolia*. Manila.

———. 2000. *Financial Management and Governance Issues in the People's Republic of China*. Manila.

———. 2000. *Financial Management and Governance Issues in Uzbekistan*. Manila.

Alt, James E., David D. Lassen and David Skilling. 2001. Fiscal Transparency and Fiscal Policy Outcomes in OECD Countries. Paper presented at the 2001 annual meeting of the American Political Science Association.

Ball, I., T. Dale, W. D. Eggers and J. Sacco. 1999. *Reforming Financial Management in the Public Sector: Lessons US Officials Can Learn From New Zealand*. Policy Study No. 258. Los Angeles: Reason Public Policy Institute. Reason Foundation.

Blöndal, Jón R. and Jens Kromann Kristensen. 2002. Budgeting in the Netherlands. *OECD Journal on Budgeting*. Vol 1(3). pp. 43–80.

Boston, J. (ed.). 1995. *The State Under Contract*. Wellington, New Zealand: Bridget Williams Books.

Brumby, Jim, Peter Edmonds & Kim Honeyfield. 1996. Effects of public sector financial management reform in New Zealand. Paper presented at the Australasian Evaluation Society Conference, Wellington, New Zealand, 30 August.

Brumby, Jim and Marco Cangiano. 2001. Public Expenditure Management Reform and Fiscal Consolidation in OECD Countries. Paper presented at the Fifth International Conference on Institutions in Transition organized by the Slovenian Institute of

Macroeconomic Analysis and Development in Otočec, Slovenia, 13–14 July.

Buti, Marco and Gabriele Giudice. 2002. *Maastricht's Fiscal Rules at Ten: An Assessment*. European Commission.

Campos, J. E. & Pradhan, S. 1997. Evaluating public expenditure management systems: An experimental methodology with an application to the Australia and New Zealand reforms. *Journal of Policy Analysis and Management*, 16(3), 423-445.

Canadian Office of the Auditor General. 1995. *Toward Better Governance: Public Service Reform in New Zealand (1984-1994) and its Relevance to Canada*. Ottawa, Canada: Minister of Supply and Services.

Diamond, Jack. 2002. *Performance Budgeting: Is Accrual Accounting Required?* Working Paper WP/02/240. Washington, DC: IMF.

Easterly, W. 1999. *When Is Fiscal Adjustment an Illusion?* Paper 2109, World Bank Country Economics Department. Washington, DC: World Bank.

Economic and Social Research Institute. 2002. *Annual Report on 2002 National Accounts*. Cabinet Office. Government of Japan. 25 June.

Government Accounting Standards Board. 1999 June. *GASB 34 Basic Financial Statements—and Management's Discussion and Analysis—for State and Local Governments*. Washington, DC.

Gore, Albert. 1999. Remarks delivered at the Opening Session of the International REGO Conference. 14 January.

Government of the Marshall Islands. 2001. *Republic of the Marshall Islands: General Purpose Financial Statements and Independent Auditors' Report for the year ended 30 September 2000*. Majuro. 18 May.

Government of Sri Lanka. 1992. *Financial Regulations of the Government of the Democratic Socialist Republic of Sri Lanka*. Department of Government Printing: Colombo.

Hillier, Diana R. *From Cash to Accrual: The Canadian Experience in IFAC. 1996. Perspectives on Accrual Accounting*. Occasional Paper 3. New York: Public Sector Committee.

IFAC. 2003. *Cash Basis IPSAS: Financial Reporting under the Cash Basis of Accounting*. New York.

———. 2003. *The Modernization of Government Accounting in France: The Current Situation, the Issues and the Outlook.* New York: Public Sector Committee.

———. 2002. *Transition to the Accrual Basis of Accounting: Guidance for Governments and Government Entities.* Public Sector Study 14. New York: Public Sector Committee.

———. 2000. *Government Financial Reporting: Accounting Issues and Practices.* Study No. 11. New York: Public Sector Committee

———. 1996. *Perspectives on Accrual Accounting.* Occasional Paper 3. New York: Public Sector Committee.

———. 1994. *Implementing Accrual Accounting in Government: The New Zealand Experience.* Occasional Paper 1. Prepared by Ken Warren of NZ Treasury. October. New York: Public Sector Committee.

IMF. 2002. *Government Finance Statistics 2001 Companion Material.* Washington, DC.

———. 2001. *Government Finance Statistics Manual.* Washington, DC.

———. 2001. *Manual on Fiscal Transparency.* Washington, DC: Fiscal Affairs Department.

Jiwei, Lou (First Vice Minister, Ministry of Finance). 2002. Government Budgeting and Accounting Reform in China. *OECD Journal on Budgeting.* Vol 2(1). December. pp. 51–80.

Kelsey, J. 1995. *The New Zealand Experiment: A World Model for Structural Adjustment?* Auckland University Press/Bridget Williams Books.

Kraft, Evan and Tihomir Stucka. 2002. *Fiscal Consolidation, External Competitiveness and Monetary Policy: A Reply to the WIIW.* May. Zagreb: Croatian National Bank.

Lihua, Dong (National Bureau of Statistics). 2001. The Status of Implementation of the 1993 SNA in China. Paper presented at workshop on ADB TA No. 5874-REG: Rebasing and Linking of NAS, 13-16 February. p. 3.

Lüder, Klaus. 2002. Government Budgeting and Accounting Reform in Germany. *OECD Journal on Budgeting.* Vol 2(1). December. pp. 224–242.

Matheson, Alex. 2002. Better Public Sector Governance: The Rationale for Budgeting and Accounting Reform in Western Nations. *OECD Journal on Budgeting.* Vol 2(1). December. pp. 44–45.

Mellor, Thuy. 1996. Why Governments Should Produce Balance Sheets. *Australian Journal of Public Administration.* 55(1). March. pp. 78-81.

Montesinos, Vicente. 2002. Government Budgeting and Accounting Reform in Spain. *OECD Journal on Budgeting.* Vol 2(1). December. pp. 333–354.

New Zealand Treasury. 1993. Reports of the Fiscal Indicators Working Party. Unpublished documents.

Nobes, Christopher and Robert Parker. 1995. *Comparative International Accounting:* Fourth Edition: Prentice Hall.

OECD. 2002. *Accrual Accounting and Budgeting: Key Issues and Recent Developments.* PUMA/SBO (2002)10. Paris.

———. 2002. Models of Public Budgeting and Accounting Reform. *OECD Journal on Budgeting.* Vol 2(1). December.

———. 2002. *PUMA Database Reports.* August. Paris.

———. 2000. *Focus.* December (18).

———. 1999. *Focus.* 12 March.

———. 1998. *Public Management Developments in Austria:* Update 1998. Paris.

———. 1997. Iceland's budget and financial accounting reform. http://www1.oecd.org/puma/focus/compend/is.htm#Iceland's%20budget%20and%20financial%20accounting%20reform [accessed on 12 December 2002].

Pant, Bishnu D. 2002. Statistical Capacity Building: An ADB Perspective for a Fresh Approach. Presented at the ADB / PARIS21 High Level Forum on Statistical Capacity Building for ASEAN Countries. Manila, 7-9 November.

Perotti, Roberto. 2002. Estimating the Effects of Fiscal Policy in OECD Countries. Paper presented at the ISOM Conference, Frankfurt, 14-15 June.

Pobre, Hermogenes P. and Araceli Bernal-Magno. 1987. *Government Accounting.* Manila.

Porterba, James M. and Kim Rueben. State Fiscal Institutions and the US Municipal Bond Market, in Porterba, James M. and Jurgen von Hagen (eds). 1999. *Fiscal Institutions and Fiscal Performance.* A National Bureau of Economic Research Conference Report. University of Chicago Press. pp. 181–208.

Public Sector Performance (NZ) Ltd. April 1999. Final Report on TA No. 2931-MON: Program Preparation for Governance Reforms: Status Assessment of Pilot Agencies. Vol III(3). p. 16.

Richardson, Ruth. Opening and Balancing the Books: The New Zealand Experience in IFAC. 1996. *Perspectives on Accrual Accounting.* Occasional Paper 3. New York: Public Sector Committee.

Robinson, Marc. 2001. The Treatment of Revaluations in Accrual-Based Government Accounts. *Journal of Accounting, Accountability and Performance.* Vol 7(2).

Schiavo-Campo, Salvatore and Daniel Tommasi (eds.). 1999. *Managing Government Expenditure.* Manila: ADB.

Schick, Allen. 2002. Fiscal Rules and Fiscal Risks. Presentation at the World Bank Training Course, 21 May.

———. 1998. Why Most Developing Countries Should Not Try New Zealand's Reforms. *World Bank Research Observer.* February.

———. 1998. *A Contemporary Approach to Public Expenditure Management.* Washington, DC: World Bank.

———. 1996. *The Spirit of Reform: Managing the New Zealand State Sector in a Time of Change.* Wellington, New Zealand: State Services Commission.

Schwartz, H. M. 1997. Reinvention and retrenchment: Lessons from the application of the New Zealand model to Alberta, Canada, *Journal of Policy Analysis and Management,* 16(3), 405-421.

Scott, Graham, Ian Ball and Tony Dale. 1997. New Zealand's Public Sector Management Reform: Implications for the United States. *Journal of Policy Analysis and Management* 16.3: 357-381.

Stace, D. & Norman, R. 1995. *Re-invented Government: The New Zealand Experience.* Centre for Corporate Change, Australian Graduate School of Management, University of New South Wales, CCC Paper No. 050.

Ström, Sten. Full Accrual Government Accounting in Sweden, in IFAC. 1996. *Perspectives on Accrual Accounting.* Occasional Paper 3. New York: Public Sector Committee. p. 26-30.

Swedish National Financial Authority (Ekonomistyrningsverket). 2001. *Accrual Accounting in Swedish Central Government.* May. Stockholm.

US Government. 2002. *2001 Financial Report of the United States Government.* Washington, DC.

UN. 1993. *System of National Accounts (SNA) Manual.* New York.

Vatuloka, Eroni and Greg E. Shailer. 2000. Preferences for the Regulation and Monitoring of Fijian Government Accounting. *Asian Accounting Review.* Vol(8). No. 2.

Virola, Romulo A. and Estrella V. Domingo. 2001. Changing the Philippine National Accounts Series. Paper presented at the concluding workshop on RETA 5874: Rebasing and Linking of National Accounts Series, held in Bangkok, Thailand, 13-16 February.

Warren, Ken. 2000. The Impact of GAAP on Fiscal Decision Making: A Review of Ten Years Experience with accrual and output-based budgets in New Zealand. Paper prepared for the Australasian Treasury Officers Conference. October.

World Bank. 1998. *Public Expenditure Management Handbook.* Washington, DC.

Appendix 1. International Public Sector Accounting Standards

As of January 2003, the International Federation of Accountants Public Sector Committee (PSC) had issued the following International Public Sector Accounting Standards (IPSAS):

- IPSAS 1 *Presentation of Financial Statements* prescribes the overall considerations for the presentation of financial statements, guidance for the structure and minimum requirements for the content of financial statements prepared under the accrual accounting basis.

- IPSAS 2 *Cash Flow Statements* requires the provision of information about the historical changes in cash and cash equivalents of an entity by means of a cash flow statement that classifies cash flows during the period from operating, investing and financing activities. Cash flow information allows users to ascertain how a public sector entity raised the cash it required to fund its activities and the manner in which that cash was used.

- IPSAS 3 *Net Surplus or Deficit for the Period, Fundamental Errors and Changes in Accounting Policies* requires the classification and disclosure of extraordinary items and the separate disclosure of certain items in the financial statements. It also specifies the accounting treatment for changes in accounting estimates, changes in accounting policies and the correction of fundamental errors.

- IPSAS 4 *The Effect of Changes in Foreign Exchange Rates* deals with accounting for foreign currency transactions and foreign operations. IPSAS 4 sets out the requirements for deciding which exchange rate to use and how to recognize in the financial statements the financial effect of changes in exchange rates.

- IPSAS 5 *Borrowing Costs* prescribes the accounting treatment for borrowing costs and generally requires the immediate expensing of borrowing costs. However, the Standard permits, as an allowed alternative treatment, the capitalization of borrowing costs that are directly attributable to the acquisition, construction or production of a qualifying asset.

- IPSAS 6 *Consolidated Financial Statements and Accounting for Controlled Entities* requires all controlling entities to prepare consolidated financial statements, which consolidate all controlled entities on a line-by-line basis. The Standard also contains a detailed discussion of the concept of control as it applies in the public sector and guidance on determining whether control exists for financial reporting purposes.

- IPSAS 7 *Accounting for Investments in Associates* requires all investments in associates to be accounted for in the consolidated financial statements using the equity method of accounting, except when the investment is acquired and held exclusively with a view to its disposal in the near future in which case the cost method is required.

- IPSAS 8 *Financial Reporting of Interests in Joint Ventures* specifies proportionate consolidation as the benchmark treatment for accounting for such joint ventures entered into by public sector entities. IPSAS 8 also permits—as an allowed alternative—joint ventures to be accounted for using the equity method of accounting.

- IPSAS 9 *Revenue from Exchange Transactions* establishes the conditions for the recognition of revenue arising from exchange transactions, requires such revenue to be measured at the fair value of the consideration received or receivable and includes disclosure requirements.

- IPSAS 10 *Financial Reporting in Hyperinflationary Economies* describes the characteristics of a hyperinflationary economy and requires financial statements of entities that operate in such economies to be restated.

- IPSAS 11 *Construction Contracts* defines construction contracts, establishes requirements for the recognition of revenues and expenses arising from such contracts and identifies certain disclosure requirements.

- IPSAS 12 *Inventories* defines inventories, establishes measurement requirements for inventories (including those inventories which are held for distribution at no or nominal charge) under the historical cost system and includes disclosure requirements.

- IPSAS 13 *Leases* prescribes the appropriate accounting policies and disclosures to apply in relation to finance and operating leases.

- IPSAS 14 *Events After the Reporting Date* prescribes when entities should adjust their financial statements for events after the reporting date; and disclosures that entities should give about the date when the financial statements were authorized for issue and about events after the reporting date.

- IPSAS 15 *Financial Instruments: Disclosure and Presentation* provides guidance on the significance of on-balance-sheet and off-balance-sheet financial instruments to a government's or other public sector entity's financial position, performance and cash flows.

- IPSAS 16 *Investment Property* prescribes the accounting treatment for investment property and related disclosure requirements.

- IPSAS 17 *Property, Plant and Equipment* describes the principal issues in accounting for property, plant and equipment, including the timing of recognition of the assets, the determination of their carrying amounts and the depreciation charges to be recognized in relation to them.

- IPSAS 18 *Segment Reporting* establishes principles for reporting financial information about distinguishable activities of a government or other public sector entity.

- IPSAS 19 *Provisions, Contingent Liabilities and Contingent Assets* defines provisions, contingent liabilities and contingent assets; and identifies the circumstances in which provisions should be recognized, how they should be measured and the disclosures that should be made about them. The Standard also requires that certain information be disclosed about contingent liabilities and contingent assets in the notes to the financial statements to enable users to understand their nature, timing, and amount.

- IPSAS 20 *Related Party Disclosures* requires the disclosure of the existence of related party relationships where control exists and the disclosure of information about transactions between the entity and its related parties in certain circumstances. This information is required for accountability purposes and to facilitate a better understanding of the financial position and performance of the reporting entity. The principal issues in disclosing information about related parties are identifying which parties control or significantly influence the reporting entity and determining what information should be disclosed about transactions with those parties.

- Cash Basis IPSAS *Financial Reporting under the Cash Basis of Accounting* includes requirements for a government and government entity to report all cash receipts, payments and balances that it controls and to disclose information about amounts settled on its behalf by third parties. It encourages note disclosure of additional information about, for example, assets, liabilities, transactions administered on behalf of others and whether budgeted amounts have been exceeded.

Appendix 2. Government-Specific Accounting Issues

This appendix describes several public sector-specific accounting issues.[89] These issues are equally relevant to developed and developing countries.

The Reporting Entity and Aggregate Consolidation

Governments comprise different levels and sectors (see Figure 1 on page 4), which complicates reporting entity definitions. The primary test is that of control. In particular, the treatment of non-central (i.e., local governments) for consolidation purposes varies depending on historical and constitutional arrangements. For instance, whereas the United Kingdom intends to consolidate local governments into the aggregate government financial statements, the United States (US) does not.

The Enron collapse illustrated problems defining the reporting entity for accounting purposes—i.e., a significant proportion of Enron's liabilities were held by special purpose entities, which (arguably) were not required to be consolidated under US generally accepted accounting principles.

Infrastructure Assets

Infrastructure assets mainly comprise highways and other network assets (such as water supply systems). These assets usually have significant values. Key accounting issues involving these assets include:

- These assets have very long useful lives, which makes decisions about appropriate depreciation treatments difficult. In response, a few countries do not depreciate infrastructure assets, but certify that they are being maintained to such an extent that they have infinite life spans.

- It is often difficult to estimate the original acquisition costs of these assets due to their old age and difficulties in separating out original investments and maintenance costs.

- Valuation methods have an exceptionally high impact on these assets.

- Recognizing and depreciating infrastructure assets can have two major policy impacts: (i) it can highlight the need for often-neglected

---

[89] This section is based on the following paper: OECD. 2002. *Accrual Accounting and Budgeting: Key Issues and Recent Developments*. Paris.

maintenance expenditures; and (ii) depending on financial arrangements, the implicit effect of requiring resources to be set aside for asset replacement can significantly reduce the amount of expenditures available for other activities.

Social Insurance Programs

The treatment of social insurance programs—such as general old-age pension programs—is a contentious issue in an accrual environment. This does not refer to the treatment of government employees' pension programs; these are contractual obligations and their treatment as a liability is clear-cut. Some believe certain obligations to provide future benefits under social insurance programs should be treated as government liabilities; others do not.

Valuation Issues

The traditional valuation basis has been historic cost (e.g., the original asset purchase price). However, there is a trend to fair value accounting. Conceptually, current valuations are generally viewed as superior, but practical considerations often lead to use of the historic cost approach. Both the System of National Accounts (SNA) and Governance Finance Statistics (GFS) require that assets be revalued.

Military Assets

There have been two schools of thought regarding military assets (such as warplanes). On one hand, some governments capitalize and depreciate these assets. Conversely, some countries expense military asset purchases.

Heritage Assets

Heritage assets comprise historical buildings, monuments and archaeological sites; and museum, gallery and archive collections. International Public Sector Accounting Standard (IPSAS) 17 *Property, Plant and Equipment* allows, but does not require, heritage assets to be recognized (accounted for). Conversely, SNA 1993 and GFS require historic monuments to be identified and valued:

"Buildings and structures that are also historic monuments are included within the appropriate category of buildings and structures. Historic monuments are structures or sites of special archaeological, historic, or cultural significance. They are usually accessible to the general public, and visitors are often charged for admission to the monuments or their vicinity. General government units typically use historic monuments to produce cultural or entertainment-type services. They can be valued directly, however, only when their significance has been recognized by someone other than the owner, typically by a sale or a formal appraisal. Historic monuments should be valued at the most recent sale price, updated, if need be, by a general price index. If no sale price is available, then an alternative valuation, such as an insurance appraisal, should be used."[90]

The practice of some countries in recognizing and valuing their heritage assets creates controversy. First, opponents contend that a monetary value cannot be placed on something whose value is inherently cultural and not monetary. Second, the usefulness of reporting heritage asset values in government balance sheets has been questioned. Conversely, supporters argue that there are benefits to be gained in terms of improved asset stewardship. In any case, for most countries, heritage assets will not comprise a significant proportion of a government's assets.

---

[90] IMF. 2001. *Government Finance Statistics Manual.* Washington, DC. para 7.39.

Appendix 3. Cost-Benefit Analysis of the New Zealand Adoption of Accrual Accounting

This appendix presents a cost-benefit analysis of the New Zealand implementation of accrual budgeting and accounting. The analysis presented in the table next page was prepared on the following basis:

- An attempt is made to quantify the benefits of enhanced credibility, brought about by the introduction of accrual accounting, and its impact on borrowing costs. Although mention has been made of evidence from the United States (US) that "states that use accrual information borrow at better terms than those states that use solely cash information,"[91] we were unable to locate the evidence.[92] However, in the absence of the supporting empirical evidence, it is (arguably) assumed that (i) implicit savings on borrowing costs caused by the introduction of accrual accounting are 0.04%; and (ii) benefits begin to be realized in year 4.

- No attempt is made to estimate the following benefits as their effects cannot be accurately quantified:
    - better estimates of the macroeconomic impact of government fiscal policy;
    - better information on payment arrears;
    - more comprehensive information;
    - improved liquidity management;
    - improved management of non-financial assets;
    - consistency with other macroeconomic statistical systems;
    - enhanced simplicity and understandability;
    - reduced opportunities for manipulation;
    - enhanced comparability;

---

[91] Brumby, Jim in Schiavo-Campo, Salvatore and Daniel Tommasi (eds.). 1999. *Managing Government Expenditure*. Manila: ADB. p. 360.

[92] In an attempt to hunt down the cited study, the authors of the following related studies were contacted:
- Alt, James E., David D. Lassen and David Skilling. 2001. Fiscal Transparency and Fiscal Policy Outcomes in OECD Countries. Paper presented at the 2001 annual meeting of the American Political Science Association.
- Porterba, James M. and Kim Rueben. State Fiscal Institutions and the US Municipal Bond Market, in Porterba, James M. and Jurgen von Hagen (eds). 1999. *Fiscal Institutions and Fiscal Performance*. A National Bureau of Economic Research Conference Report. University of Chicago Press. pp. 181–208.

- o better information on the sustainability of fiscal policy settings;
- o better information on the macroeconomic Impacts of current and capital flows;
- o improved information to support fiscal strategy decisions;
- o improved measures of intergenerational equity;
- o improved accountability;
- o improved resource management;
- o better information on future commitments;
- o better information to support liquidity management;
- o better information to support pricing decisions; and
- o improved access to financial personnel and financial information systems.

- A static analysis has been prepared—debt levels are assumed to remain constant.

- The internal rate of return (IRR) calculation is based on a 20-year period.

- Implementation costs are estimated, based on an NZ Audit Office study that estimated the total cost of financial-management reform for the period 1987–92 was $99 million (NZ$160-180 million) or about 0.1% of government expenses during this period. This study included direct costs such as (i) financial management information system (FMIS) purchases and implementation; and (ii) consulting expenses. It also estimated indirect expenses, such as staff time.[93] Implementation costs are phased over a 5-year period, reflecting implementation activities.

---

[93] Cited in: Scott, Graham, Ian Ball and Tony Dale (Summer 1997). New Zealand's Public Sector Management Reform: Implications for the United States. *Journal of Policy Analysis and Management* 16.3: 357-381

Cost-Benefit Analysis of Country Implementation

		Year								
		1987	1988	1989	1990	1991	1992	1993	1994 ...	2006
Quantifiable Benefits: Enhanced credibility and its impact on borrowing costs:										
Gross Debt Outstanding ($ million)	50,000									
Transparency effect on borrowing rates	0.04%									
Implicit interest saving	20									
Benefits (reduction in borrowing costs; assumed that benefits begin in year 4)		..	..	..	10	20	20	20	20	20
...		...	...	...	...	...	...	...	...	...
Total Quantifiable Benefits		..	..	..	10	20	20	20	20	20
Quantifiable Implementation Costs										
Based on NZ Audit Office study		36	54	54	18	18	..	..	..	..
Total Quantifiable Costs		36	54	54	18	18	..	..	..	..
Net Benefits/(Costs)		-36	-54	-54	-8	2	20	20	20	20
Internal Rate of Return (IRR, %)	7%									

According to the analysis, the implementation would yield an internal rate of return of +7%. This is likely to be a very conservative analysis given the following considerations:

- The analysis **excludes almost all benefits** because they cannot be accurately quantified (see above).

- The interest-rate adjustment factor used applies in a low-interest-rate environment (US municipal government). However, the **interest-rate benefits are likely to be understated** because prevailing New Zealand interest rates were higher.

- The **implementation costs are overstated** because they include the entire estimated costs of New Zealand's financial management reforms; including for instance, the costs associated with performance contracting and output specification.

Appendix 4. OECD Implementation Experiences

This appendix describes the approaches of 4 OECD member countries to implementing accrual budgeting and accounting.

Canada

Throughout the 1980s, Canadian provincial governments significantly changed their financial reporting practices, moving from cash to accrual accounting and from separate account reporting to consolidated financial statements.[94]

In 1995, Canada established the Financial Information Strategy (FIS) with the goal of bringing FIS systems on-line by 1 April 2001 (which was met). This involved changing the way government departments and agencies kept their books for more than 100 years.

For consolidated government financial reporting at a federal level, monthly financial statements will continue on a modified accrual basis until publication of the annual audited 2001-2002 financial statements on a full accrual basis. The Canadian Parliament is currently considering how it might introduce accrual-based appropriations.

Germany

German public sector financial management reforms are largely a direct consequence of attempts to reform the public sector through privatization, corporatization, decentralization, devolved management, competition and the output performance orientation. The changes have been relatively slow and careful to avoid uncertainty. They were first introduced in local government, and later in Länder (state) and federal government. They focused on budgeting and managerial accounting.[95]

The step-by-step approach involved pilot projects. This avoided the need to amend the legal basis of financial management in the early phase of the reform process. On one hand, this approach resulted in many projects with poor conceptual bases, unclear objectives, insufficient coordination and an absence of systematic outcomes evaluations. On the other hand, the

---

[94] Hillier, Diana R. *From Cash to Accrual: The Canadian Experience*, in International Federation of Accountants (IFAC). 1996. Perspectives on Accrual Accounting. Occasional Paper 3. New York: Public Sector Committee.

[95] Lüder, Klaus. 2002. Government Budgeting and Accounting Reform in Germany. *OECD Journal on Budgeting*. Vol 2(1). December. pp. 224–242.

pilot project approach is beneficial in the early phase of public sector financial management reform because it enables jurisdictions to test new ideas, particularly in countries with very stringent and detailed legal provisions for public sector financial management.

There is, however, a danger that the reform process may never get beyond piloting. To combat this danger, sufficient conceptual guidance, clear objectives and a limited time frame are crucial for pilot projects to be a useful element in the reform process.

Länder and federal governments are following local governments in changing their financial management systems. But a majority of them still prefer an additive reform approach—they intend to supplement the existing system with new elements, such as output budgeting and cost and performance accounting. A complete substitution of an accrual budgeting and accounting system for the traditional system is still inconceivable for most of these governments and their political leaders.

Sweden

Following a gradual 2-year implementation, accrual accounting was fully implemented in the Swedish central Government from 1 July 1993. Although it involved a significant effort, the implementation was problem-free for two reasons. First, no organizational changes were necessary—the structure of Swedish Government suited the implementation of accruals and results-based management. Second, accruals were initially only implemented for agency accounting and for whole-of-government reporting, but not for budgetary (appropriation) purposes. This reduced complications.[96]

Implementation efforts involved (i) adjusting accounting systems; (ii) developing accounting policies; (iii) altering processes and procedures; and (iv) executing a significant information, education and training campaign. The costs of these activities were not easily identifiable.[97]

Heritage assets were not included (due to valuation difficulties) and defense assets were initially expensed rather than capitalized.[98]

---

[96] Swedish National Financial Authority (Ekonomistyrningsverket). 2001. *Accrual Accounting in Swedish Central Government.* May. Stockholm.
[97] Ibid.
[98] Ström, Sten. Full Accrual Government Accounting in Sweden, in IFAC. 1996. *Perspectives on Accrual Accounting.* Occasional Paper 3. New York: Public Sector Committee. p. 26-30.

Before implementation, most agencies used a centralized **computerized accounting system** that was introduced in the late 1960s. This system was modified to handle accruals. In addition, a new system was made available to agencies. The new system is a commercial accounting system widely used by private companies throughout the world. The introduction of the new system made it possible to decentralize government accounting.[99]

Government **accounting policies** began to be aligned with the private sector in the 1980s. However, the policies were not fully accrual-based until 1993. Moreover, certain adaptations were made to reflect specific government needs.

Education, training and communication activities were conducted before implementation began. First, materials explaining the changes were produced. Second, training for financial personnel was conducted, mainly through seminars. Finally, a National Financial Authority staff member was assigned to each agency as a contact point and advisor.

Notably, the professionalism of formerly lowly-ranked **accounting personnel** was raised considerably and it is now possible to recruit trained accountants into government agencies.

United Kingdom

The United Kingdom has adopted accrual accounting at the agency level and is looking to produce aggregate consolidated financial statements for 2006. It plans to prepare consolidated financial statements in a staged manner:

- Stage 1 will involve consolidating the unaudited central government accounts using 2001-02 National Accounts (System of National Accounts) information.
- Stage 2 will involve consolidating accrual 2003-2004 central government accounts.
- Stage 3 will involve a whole-of-government accounts consolidation for 2005-2006.

---

[99] Swedish National Financial Authority (Ekonomistyrningsverket). 2001. *Accrual Accounting in Swedish Central Government*. May. Stockholm.

Appendix 5. Useful Internet Sites and Resources

Useful Internet Sites

Government Accounting Standards Board (US)	GASB	www.gasb.org
Intergovernmental Working Group of Experts on International Standards of Accounting and Reporting of the United Nations Conference on Trade and Development (UNCTAD)	ISAR	www.unctad.org/isar/
International Accounting Standards Board	IASB	www.iasb.org.uk
International Federation of Accountants	IFAC	www.ifac.org
International Organization of Supreme Audit Institutions	INTOSAI	www.intosai.org

International Public Sector Material

As of June 2002, the International Federation of Accountants Public Sector Committee had released the following studies and guidance materials.

International Public Sector Studies

- Study 1 *Financial Reporting by National Governments* addresses the fundamental underpinnings of governmental financial reporting.

- Study 2 *Elements of the Financial Statements of National Governments* considers the elements (types or classes of financial information) to be reported in financial statements prepared under the different bases of accounting that may be employed by national governments and their major units and the way in which those elements may be defined.

- Study 3 *Auditing for Compliance with Authorities: A Public Sector Perspective* addresses aspects of the audit for compliance in the public sector that, in many countries, is subject to very different mandates and objectives than in the private sector.

- Study 4 *Using the Work of Other Auditors: A Public Sector Perspective* addresses using the work of other auditors, including both other external and internal auditors, in financial attest and compliance audits.

- Study 5 *Definition and Recognition of Assets* identifies and describes the variety of views that exist about whether, when, and how specific assets should be measured and reported in the public sector.

- Study 6 *Accounting for and Reporting Liabilities* provides a public sector perspective on the definition and recognition of liabilities.

- Study 7 *Performance Reporting by Government Business Enterprises* identifies principal users of performance information, considers the needs of those users and outlines forms of reporting that could be available to meet those needs.

- Study 8 *The Government Financial Reporting Entity* considers the implications of different approaches to the definition of the government financial reporting entity and different techniques for the construction of government financial reports to the achievement of objectives of financial reports.

- Study 9 *Definition and Recognition of Revenues* examines concepts, principles and issues related to the definition and recognition of revenues in the general purpose financial statements of national governments and other nonbusiness public sector entities.

- Study 10 *Definition and Recognition of Expenses and Expenditures* examines the concepts, principles and issues related to the treatment of expenses/expenditures in general purpose financial statements of governments and other nonbusiness public sector entities.

- Study 11 *Government Financial Reporting: Accounting Issues and Practices* aims to assist governments at all levels in the identification of issues associated with financial reporting (on both the cash and accrual accounting bases).

- Study 12 *Perspectives on Cost Accounting for Governments* is intended to assist government financial aid officers and other government accountants in their efforts to develop and implement cost accounting.

- Study 13 *Governance in the Public Sector* examines public sector governance issues.

- Study 14 *Transition to the Accrual Basis of Accounting: Guidance for Governments and Government Entities* is intended to help entities intending to move to the accrual basis of accounting and comply with the accrual-based International Public Sector Accounting Standards.

Occasional Papers

- No. 1 *Implementing Accrual Accounting in Government-The New Zealand Experience*

- No. 2 *Auditing Whole of Government Financial Statements-The New Zealand Experience*

- No. 3 *Perspectives on Accrual Accounting* aims to inform readers about a range of perspectives on accrual accounting from a number of contributors who have experience in implementing accounting reform in the public sector or who have observed its progress.

- No. 4 *The Delegation of Public Services in France-An Original Method of Public Administration: Delegated Public Service* describes the specific framework designed in France to manage the relationship between a government entity and a private sector entity contracted to deliver a certain service, and to ensure an adequate level of information and accountability.

- No. 5 *Resource Accounting: Framework of Accounting Standard Setting in the United Kingdom Central Government Sector* considers the experiences of the United Kingdom, which decided to move to an accrual basis for both budgeting and financial reporting in 1995.

- No. 6 *The Modernization of Government Accounting in France: The Current Situation, the Issues and the Outlook.*

Appendix 6. Suggested Readings

The following publications provide useful information on accrual budgeting and accounting issues in government.

Diamond, Jack. 2002. *Performance Budgeting: Is Accrual Accounting Required?* Working Paper WP/02/240. Washington, DC: IMF.

IFAC. 2002. *Transition to the Accrual Basis of Accounting: Guidance for Governments and Government Entities.* Public Sector Study 14. New York.

———. 1996. *Perspectives on Accrual Accounting.* Occasional Paper 3. New York: Public Sector Committee.

IMF. 2002. *Government Finance Statistics 2001 Companion Material.* Washington, DC.

———. 2001. *Manual on Fiscal Transparency.* Washington, DC: Fiscal Affairs Department.

Mellor, Thuy. 1996. Why Governments Should Produce Balance Sheets. *Australian Journal of Public Administration.* 55(1). March. pp. 78-81.

OECD. 2002. *Accrual Accounting and Budgeting: Key Issues and Recent Developments.* PUMA/SBO(2002)10. Paris.

———. 2002. Models of Public Budgeting and Accounting Reform. *OECD Journal on Budgeting.* Vol 2(1). December. pp. 5-6.

Schiavo-Campo, Salvatore and Daniel Tommasi. 1999. *Managing Government Expenditure.* Manila: Asian Development Bank.

Warren, Ken. 2000. *The Impact of GAAP on Fiscal Decision Making: A Review of Ten Years Experience with Accrual and Output-based Budgets in New Zealand.* Paper prepared for the Australasian Treasury Officers Conference. October.

World Bank. 1998. *Public Expenditure Management Handbook.* Washington, DC.